Ketogenic Diet Cookbook For Instant Pot

Over 230 Amazingly Quick, Simple And Delicous Instant Pot Recipes To Lose Weight Rapidly And Improve Your Life(Electric Pressure Cooker Cookbook)

Jack Toll

Table of Contents

Introduction

I would like to thank and congratulate you for purchasing this book *"Ketogenic Diet Cookbook For Instant Pot-Over 230 Amazingly Quick, Simple And Delicous Instant Pot Recipes To Lose Weight Rapidly And Improve Your Life(Electric Pressure Cooker Cookbook)."*

This book is suitable for people of all shapes and sizes! My hope is that this collection of healthy ketogenic instant pot recipes is going to help lead you and your loved ones to healthier lifestyle. They are all healthy and will do good to your weight loss goal! You will like them!

I know that it can be hard to lose weight, but when you find a way to do it that you will enjoy you are much more likely to succeed in your weight loss goals. I am sure you want to be healthy, avoid illness, and be a healthy weight, while getting to enjoy delicious foods. Well the good news is you can get healthy and enjoy your meals at the same time when you use this collection of ketogenic recipes.

Are you like many of us and find yourself so busy with work and other things in life that you often have no time to cook? With the wonderful instant pot, you will be able to toss the ingredients into your instant pot, allow the cooking process to work its magic and before you know it you will have a delicious healthy meal to enjoy! I hope you will have plenty of healthy meals using this book as an easy guide on using the instant pot and keto diet!

Chapter 1. All About the Ketogenic Diet?

One of the most popular low-carb diets available today is the 'ketogenic diet.' Due to the many advantages that the ketogenic diet offers many people are turning to it. There are multiple benefits to the ketogenic diet, it is a very powerful way to lose weight while leading you towards healthy eating habits and lifestyle which most fad diets do not. You will learn all you need to know about the ketogenic diet in this chapter.

What is the Ketogenic Diet?

The ketogenic diet is a low-carbohydrate, moderate protein, high-fat diet. It is a diet that concentrates on decreasing your carbohydrate intake and replacing it with healthy fats and proteins. You body in it's normal functions burns carbohydrates to convert into glucose, which is in turn carried throughout your body and is essential for brain fuel. However, when your body has low amounts of carbohydrates, your liver will begin to convert fat into fatty acids and ketone bodies. The ketone bodies replace glucose, moving into your brain where they provide the primary energy source.

The ketogenic diet was created so that you could reach a state of *ketosis*. Ketosis is a metabolic state in which your body produces ketones. Your liver produces ketones that are used as fuel for your body and brain instead of glucose. You must consume a substantial amount of carbs to make ketones, with a minimum amount of proteins. There is a ratio of 4:1 by weight of fat to combined protein and carbohydrate with the traditional ketogenic diet. You can accomplish this when you eliminate high-carbohydrate foods from your diet, such as starchy vegetables, breads, fruits, pasta, grains, and sugar while you boost the consumption of foods high in fats, such as cream, nuts, and butter. The ketogenic diet is a low-carb diet that will help to burn body fat.

Benefits of Ketogenic Diet

There are many benefits that are connected to the ketogenic diet. For starters, it has been used to help in treating epileptic seizures and various other diseases, including Alzheimer's and cancer.

The ketogenic diet can be used to improve and enhance your overall health by preventing and helping to control substances within your body. Some of the benefits of the ketogenic diet are as follows:

Weight Loss

Carbs are kept to a minimum with the ketogenic diet plan. There has been research that has proven that ketogenic practitioners lose weight faster and easier compared to other people. Why? Simply because the number of carbohydrates on a ketogenic diet plan will be drastically reduced in each meal.

The excess water stored in your body will begin to shed when you begin to consume fewer carbohydrates. This will in turn reduce the levels of insulin in your body, which would directly impact your sodium levels, which in turn results in weight loss.

Decrease in Blood Pressure

If you suffer from high blood pressure or hypertension, this could make you more likely to develop several health issues, like kidney failure, heart disease, or stroke. One of the best ways to help reduce your blood pressure is to go onto a low-carb diet. Your exposure to diseases will decrease when you are on a low-carb diet plan. Research has also revealed that when you reduce consumption of carbohydrates it leads to a significant reduction in blood pressure, thus in turn helping to reduce your chances of developing various diseases.

Improve Your HDL Cholesterol

A special kind of protein known as HDL cholesterol runs by transferring the 'bad cholesterol' from your body and into your liver, where the cholesterol is either exerted or reused. When your HDL cholesterol is high, your cholesterol deposits within your blood vessel walls, thus helping to prevent blockage that could erupt or encourage heart disease or heart pain. Diets such as the ketogenic diet that are high in fat are known for raising your blood vessels with HDL, this means that you will reduce the risk of developing cardiovascular disease.

Diminishes Your Appetite

When you follow a low-carb diet it can help to alleviate your hunger. One of the main reasons people often drop diet plans is because of the feeling of being hungry. However, when you follow a low-carb diet, your appetite will become reduced. The more carbs that you cut out of your diet the more you will add protein and healthy fats. Which will result in consuming fewer calories without eating less.

Improve Digestion

The ketogenic diet contains low carbs, low sugars, and low grains, which can improve your digestion immensely. When you are on a diet that largely consists of carbs and sugars, this can result in gas, stomach pains, bloating and constipation. By reducing carbohydrates and sugars in your diet can help to renew your digestive system.

Improves Mental Health

The ketone bodies that are released when you follow a ketogenic diet plan have been directly linked to mental health. Research has revealed that increased ketone levels can lead to stabilization of neurotransmitters, like serotonin and dopamine. With this stabilization it can help fight depression, mood swings, and other psychological issues.

Increases Energy

A ketogenic diet can increase your energy levels in numerous ways. It will help to increase your mitochondrial function, while at the same time decreases the harmful radicals inside your body. Resulting you feeling more energetic and revitalized.

Reduces Triglycerides

Triglycerides are also referred to as fat molecules. There has been links with increased levels of triglycerides to heart health. Thus, it is extremely important to lower triglyceride levels, which you can accomplish through the ketogenic diet. The more carbohydrates that you are consuming will result in more triglycerides in your blood, which in turn can trigger heart disease. Cutting or reducing the number of carbohydrates you are consuming will reduce the number of triglycerides in your body.

Why You Can Lose Weight Faster on the Ketogenic Diet than Other Diets

One of the largest health epidemics in the world is obesity. Many people try multiple methods to try and fight against their obesity, but many fad diets are not successful for most people who have tried them. If you truly want to overcome obesity and lose weight, you must make some positive changes in your diet. The ketogenic diet has worked for many people, helping them to preserve muscle mass, and shed excess fat, without putting much effort into it. The main purpose of the ketogenic diet is to place your body in a state of glycogen deprivation and maintain a state of *ketosis,* which is great for weight-loss. Generally, with carb-based diets, carbohydrates are converted into glucose, which in turn is used as the main source of fuel for your body and brain. The excess glucose is then converted into glycogen and stored in your liver for later use. When the glycogen steers are full in your body, the excess is stored as fat, thus leading to weight gain.

The main cause of weight gain is not eating fats, but is the excessive consumption of carbs. When you reduce your carb intake and increase your fat intake, your body will change from burning carbs for energy to burning fats for energy. This will lead to the excess fat stored in your body being burnt as your energy source, thus leading to weight-loss.

The foods that you will eat while on the ketogenic diet will help to suppress your appetite, like fats and proteins, which are filling. You will stay fuller longer and thus will feel the urge to eat less often.

What Happens While on the Ketogenic Diet to Your Body?

Ketosis is why the ketogenic diet is so efficient when it comes to improving your health and well-being, gaining more energy, lowering health risks and mental clarity. During *ketosis* your body produces ketones to provide energy for your brain and body. Normally, your body breaks down carbohydrates and turns them into glucose for its energy source or fuel. But, when you change to a ketogenic diet, your body will begin to go from storing carbohydrates to burning stored fat.

Eventually, overtime your body will adapt to this new eating regime, when you will enter ketosis. You may experience some small side effects during your transitioning period to the ketogenic lifestyle. When your body enters the ketogenic diet, here is what could happen:

Ketogenic Flu

During your first week into the ketogenic diet, it could be challenging for you. Your body could be very dependent on glucose for its main energy, so it will need to transition to use ketones for fuel. You could begin to feel unmotivated, tired, and lethargic; this is often caused due to salt deficiency and dehydration that is promoted by the temporary increase in urinating. It also suggests that your body is going to need more time to adjust to the new ingredients it is digesting and the ingredients it is not used to consuming.

Some symptoms you could experience with Keto flu:
- Nausea
- Brain Fogginess
- Insomnia
- Dizziness
- Heart Palpitations
- Coughing
- Sniffles
- Irritability
- Cravings

To help you to cope with ketogenic flu, you should increase your salt and water intake, as this can help to prevent you from feeling tired and lousy.

Bad Breath

You might encounter bad breath while you are under the ketogenic diet. It is not because the foods you will be consuming will cause bad breath. However, bad breath is a common sign of ketosis because of the elevated levels of ketones in your blood. It is caused by a specific ketone known as acetone. This ketone usually leaves your body through your urine and breath, thus creating stinky breath.

But not to worry because this symptom will only last a brief time. As with the feeling of fatigue bad breath will go away once your body has totally adapted to the ketogenic diet. While you are waiting for your body to make the full transition you may need to use some extra mouth wash more often.

Temporary Fatigue

One of the most common side effects in entering ketosis for dieters is the feeling of being fatigued. This is mainly since your body is being deprived of carbohydrates, which is the main fuel source that your body has been accustomed to. In about a week or two when your body has fully adapted to burning fats, you will begin to feel more energized and will sense an improvement in mental clarity.

You can cope with temporary fatigue by taking vitamin supplements. One essential nutrient for your body is vitamin B5. If you do not take vitamin B5 you will feel more fatigued.

The vitamin B5 will help to boost your adrenaline by increasing metabolism with more energy. You can go to a health store and purchase some vitamin B5, it will help with temporary fatigue during your ketogenic transition.

Leg Cramps

While on the ketogenic diet you could experience muscle cramps. These cramps are a symptom of hyponatremia, which occurs when your level of sodium in the blood is low. You can add an additional teaspoon of salt in your meals and keep yourself well hydrated.

Headaches

Headaches can develop when making diet changes. You could become light-headed and start having flu-like symptoms, which would develop over a few days. The headaches often happen due to mineral imbalance due changes in your diet. One way you can resolve this is to add a quarter of a teaspoon of salt to a glass of water and drink it. If you are new to the keto lifestyle, you should make sure to increase the salt and water in your daily diet for the first couple of days to help combat this effectively.

Constipation

When you first begin the keto diet, you may experience constipation within the first week of the diet, because your body may need time to adjust to this new eating regime. Eat more veggies that are loaded with fiber to help you to cope with this symptom. This will help to keep your intestines moving and will increase your bowel movements. To help fight dehydration, which is the contributing factor for constipation drink more water.

Difficulty Sleeping

Another symptom you may experience when first going on the ketogenic diet is trouble sleeping. People just start the keto lifestyle often find themselves staying up late at night, or waking up at night after cutting down on carbs. Keep in mind these symptoms are all temporary. Over time you will no longer have trouble sleeping. In fact, most people who were on the ketogenic diet had their quality of sleep improved significantly.

The symptoms listed above are the most common signs of what your body could go through when you begin the transition into your new keto lifestyle. Of course, not everyone will experience the same symptoms. Please do not feel unmotivated or discouraged about the diet. Just keep in mind that these symptoms will all pass within a few weeks and then you can begin to enjoy reaping the wonderful benefits from the ketogenic lifestyle!

The Do's and Don'ts of the Ketogenic Diet

If you are not well informed about the ketogenic diet, there are mistakes you could make that could prevent you from having good health and the benefits of this diet. To aid in enhancing your success with the ketogenic diet, here are some do's and don'ts while following the diet:

Do not increase your carb intake

The ketogenic diet is a diet based on low-carb, which means you should have a low carb intake. There is not a specific number of carbs you should have in the diet. You may find a suitable balanced number of carbs to consume, but most keto dieters manage to reach the state of ketosis by consuming between 20 to 100 grams of carbs a day.

Increase your protein intake

One of the essential nutrients your body needs is protein. Protein can help to soothe your appetite and burn fat more than any other nutrient. Protein is said to be very effective in weight-loss, increasing muscle mass, and improving your body composition.

Increase your sodium intake

When you begin to reduce your carbohydrate consumption, your insulin levels will fall, which in turn will get rid of extra sodium stored in your body, causing problems such as sodium deficiency to occur. If you find that your body is experiencing sodium deficiency, you could have symptoms such as headaches, exhaustion, and constipation.

To help get rid of this problem you need to increase your sodium intake on a keto diet. Add a teaspoon of salt daily to your meals or add a quarter of a teaspoon into a glass of water.

Don't be frightened of consuming fats

When you are on the ketogenic diet, don't be frightened of fat. Especially when you will be consuming healthy fats such as monounsaturated fats, Omega-3s, and saturated fats. The ketogenic diet encourages you to consume these types of fats. It is best to set a 60 to 70% fat intake as a limit.

For you to achieve these levels of fat, you must be consuming meat, and healthy fats, such as lard, olive oil, coconut oil, and butter daily.

Try to be patient

As humans we often seek to achieve immediate gratification. When it comes to a diet plan you may get discouraged when you do not experience the benefits immediately. The reality is that to lose weight and become healthy will take some time to achieve in a healthy manner. It will take time for your body to adjust to burning fat instead of glucose. It could take a couple of days or a couple of weeks for your body to make the transition, but be patient because it will be well worth it when you begin to reap the benefits of the healthy keto lifestyle!

Avoid eating fast food

Often when people are busy and don't have time to cook they turn to fast foods. However, you need to avoid fast foods. Eating fast foods could deter you from your keto journey, they are incredibly unhealthy, and it is best that you avoid them. There are far too many harmful chemicals and preservatives in fast foods, and some fast foods do not use real meats and cheese with hidden sugars among the ingredients.

Vital tips for a successful ketogenic journey

When first beginning your ketogenic journey, you may find it very difficult to stick to the new eating regime, even though you know it is good for your health. Often, we are influenced by unhealthy foods, which surround us and have easy access making it very difficult to pass up. When it comes to changing your diet, it is a long-term process, not something you will achieve right off the bat. Here are some vital tips to help you to have a successful ketogenic journey:

Gradually ease into following the ketogenic diet

One common mistake many make when starting the ketogenic diet is immediately eliminating carbohydrates. Doing this is not a healthy process for your body. Taking this route could cause serious health problems over the long-term. You need to give yourself time to adjust with ease into the keto lifestyle by making small but essential changes, like giving up one carb source every week or so. It is vital that you give your body time to adjust to these changes. A wonderful way to make the transition period an easier process for you is when you remove something unhealthy from your diet replace it with a healthy nutrient source. For example, if you use all-purpose flour, begin to substitute it with coconut or almond flour.

Keep hydrated by drinking lots of water

Your body is going to have a tough time keeping the proper amount of water you need when you begin the ketogenic diet. You will need to make sure that you are drinking at least eight, 8-ounce glasses of water a day, which is 2 liters. You can check if you are properly hydrated by looking at the color of your urine, if it is light yellow or clear you are properly hydrated.

Try turning your favorite foods into ketogenic foods

You can quickly become discouraged if you spend too much time thinking of foods that you are no longer allowed to eat, instead discover keto-friendly versions of your favorite dishes. I am sure you will find some of them in the 500 recipes in this cookbook!

Do not feel that you are going to have to deprive yourself of your favorite meals if you follow the ketogenic diet, but instead you will find ways to improve your diet and make it healthier.

Get advice about the ketogenic diet

You might find that you are confused or have some questions regarding the ketogenic diet, don't be afraid to reach out and ask for help. You can ask ketogenic dieters, professionals, or perhaps certified nutritionists for recipes, experiences and advice. You might be pleasantly surprised on the help and information you will receive from others.

Keep track of alcohol consumption

You can consume alcohol while you are on the ketogenic diet. However, do not over indulge and drink all the time. It is best to choose unsweetened liquors, like scotch, vodka, tequila, rum, whiskey, and reduced-carb beer.

Be aware of condiments and sauces

You need to keep in mind that not all condiments and sauces are healthy or ketogenic friendly. If you need to use condiments and sauces try to choose ones that are low in carbs, like lemon, soy sauce, mayonnaise, salad dressings, olive oil, mustard and coconut oil. If you are unsure if something is keto-friendly or not, you can ask the chef or server, if they are not sure it would be best to go without the sauce.

Don't give up but instead be patient

The ketogenic lifestyle is known for rapid weight loss, but losing weight will take time. Don't quit the diet because you are not getting fast enough results. Do not get too worked up over what the results on the scale may reveal, instead trust that the ketogenic diet will help you to lose weight in due time, you just need to remain patient.

Use vitamins and mineral salts

There are many micronutrients in foods that are high in carbohydrates, such as vitamins and minerals. When you stop consuming carbohydrates, it can cause nutritional deficiency to your body. To help fight this you should take proper vitamins that will provide your body with nutrients.

Restock pantry and fridge

The best way to begin the ketogenic diet is to get rid of unfriendly keto ingredients from your kitchen and restock with keto-friendly ingredients. This will aide you in being more attentive and will help reduce your urge to eat unfriendly keto foods. Get the supplies you will need to prepare your meals and plan ahead, this will help you to avoid any inconveniences that could cause you to lose track of your diet.

Foods that should be on your plate

The ketogenic diet has specific guidelines for you to follow. It was designed to help people who suffered from various diseases and for those looking to shed excess weight. It is a clever idea to take note of all the healthy foods that are allowed on the ketogenic diet. Below I have listed some healthy ingredients that you should include on your menu:

Vegetables

When you are on the ketogenic diet you will eat loads of vegetables. You will want to eat vegetables that are high in nutrients and low in carbohydrates. Choosing organic vegetables is best, as they will have fewer chemicals and pesticides. When you eat non-starchy vegetables, this will not cause your blood glucose levels to rise, which could throw off your ketosis. Non-starchy vegetables can also help to reduce your appetite because they are loaded with fiber. Below is a list of some of the best vegetables to eat on the ketogenic diet:

Bell Peppers

Bell peppers are very nutritious as they are packed with vitamins and fiber. Bell peppers also contain inflammatory properties than can be a useful addition on the ketogenic diet.

Zucchini

Zucchini is a wonderful low-carb vegetable and also a reliable source of vitamin A, potassium, magnesium, phosphorus, copper and folate. Zucchini also contains a high amount of omega-3 fatty acids, zinc, protein, and niacin. Including zucchini into your diet will certainly help to lead you towards an optimal healthy lifestyle.

Mushrooms

Mushrooms are a major source for anti-inflammatory properties, which can help to improve inflammation for those who suffer from metabolic problems. Mushrooms are also loaded with potassium, copper, protein, and selenium. They are also a reliable source of phosphorus, pantothenic acid, niacin, and zinc, especially when you cook them until they turn brown.

Asparagus

Asparagus is a reliable source of vitamins and minerals, including vitamins A, C, and K. Research has revealed that asparagus can help to cope with anxiety and protect mental health. It would be a healthy choice to eat roasted asparagus or add raw asparagus in your salads.

Avocados

Avocados are a reliable source of omega oils. Avocadoes can be eaten in salads or mixed with other ingredients such as yogurt and nuts. They are also high in fiber and potassium, being great for your metabolism and heart. You will often see them for sale in semi-ripened condition, so you will be able to keep them for a week or so as they ripen. Avocadoes are high in oil and mineral content, which will help to reduce your appetite and provide you with the nutrients that your body will need.

Tomatoes

There are many positive health benefits connected to tomatoes, they are a great source of vitamins A, C, and K. Tomatoes are also high in potassium, which can help reduce blood pressure and decrease stroke risks. Roasting tomatoes with olive oil can enhance the lycopene content, thus boosting its effects. It can also protect heart health and reduce the risk of cancer.

Cauliflower

Cauliflower is an excellent source of omega-3 fatty acids, dietary fiber, biotin, phosphorus, vitamins B1, B2, and B3. You can use cauliflower while preparing pizza crusts, rice, hummus, and breadsticks.

Spinach

One of the best vegetables is spinach, as it is rich in proteins, iron, and potassium. It is also very delicious and can be used in many diverse types of dishes.

Broccoli

Broccoli is a tasty vegetable that is rich in fiber, nutrients, protein, calcium, and potassium.

Lettuce

For the ketogenic lifestyle lettuce is an excellent vegetable. Lettuce contains very few carbohydrates and is a reliable source of fiber, potassium, protein, and energy. Lettuce also offers many beneficial vitamins and minerals including magnesium, iron, calcium, sodium, niacin, phosphorus, folate, vitamin B6, vitamin A, and vitamin K. You can also use lettuce leaves as a healthy ketogenic alternative to hamburger buns and taco shells.

Meat and Poultry

You can use any kind of meat on the ketogenic diet, especially if they are high in fat. Choose meat that has been grass-fed and wild animal sources. Avoid consuming sausages and hot dogs, and meat that is covered in starch or processed sauces.

Eggs

Eggs are a major source of protein and are low in carbs, especially the egg yolk.

Fats and Oils

You will need to include fats and oils in your diet since you will need to burn fat for energy when on the ketogenic diet. Instead of using vegetable oil, use olive oil, avocado oil or coconut oil, and ghee. Buy oils that are a rich source of polyunsaturated fats and have a love smoke level; these oils will retain their fatty acids. Examples of these oils are flax oil, walnut oil, hemp seed oil, and grapeseed oil.

Fish

Fish is a reliable source of protein. It is best to choose a wild fish that has been caught naturally. Such examples of these types of fish would include trout, salmon, cod, shrimp, lobster, and catfish

Fruits

You can consume fruits while on the ketogenic diet but in moderation. Some fruits could cause you to retract from reaching ketosis. Berries are the most advantageous, being packed with nutrition and having a low level of sugar.

Nuts and Seeds

Nuts contain healthy fats and nutrient such as vitamin E. Try to choose nuts that are roasted, because they will already have their anti-nutrients discarded. The best nuts and seeds to consume while on the ketogenic diet are almonds, walnuts, and macadamias. They are low in calories and will help to control your carbohydrate count.

Dairy Products

Consider consuming raw and organic dairy products while on the ketogenic diet. To prepare ketogenic meals you can use creams and cheeses. Some of the best dairy products to include in your diet are cheddar cheese, mozzarella cheese, cottage cheese, sour cream, parmesan cheese, cream cheese, Greek yogurt, and heavy whipping cream.

Foods that Should Not be on Your Plate

You must do your best to prevent and rid your body of foods that will hold you back from reaching ketosis successfully. The main foods you want to avoid are those high in carbohydrates that will not allow your body to burn fat for energy. Below is a list of foods in general that you should avoid:

Alcohol

Even though most alcohol beverages have low carbs, they can still be bad for the keto lifestyle. Alcohol can cause the fat burning process or slow it down dramatically, because your body will need to burn the alcohol before the fat. You should consider limiting your alcohol intake if you want to be successful with this diet.

Diet Soda

Diet soda pushes its big claims in not containing sugars or carbs; it instead contains artificial sweeteners which are equally as detrimental as regular sugar. With artificial sweeteners they can enhance your carbohydrate intake and can cause you to not be able to reach the metabolic state of ketosis.

Grains

Obviously, you will need to avoid foods that are made from processed grains. Grains have additives that will have a negative affect on your insulin levels. Types of these grains include pasta, bread, cookies, cakes, and pastries.

Fruits

While you are on the ketogenic diet you should avoid most fruits. Fruits contain fructose (similar to glucose), and this is not good if you want to reach ketosis. You should not only avoid fruits, but also products that are made with fresh fruit, such as extracts or juices. If you do eat fruit, make sure to do so in moderation.

Ground Vegetables

Sources of vegetables that have been picked from the ground are high in carbohydrates and prevent you from reaching ketosis. Such vegetables include onions, potatoes, beets, carrots, radishes and parsnips.

Processed Foods

You should avoid packaged or processed foods while on the ketogenic diet. These foods are stuffed with artificial additives that can lead you away from ketosis. Instead of picking processed foods choose organic and real ingredients.

These tips are all you need to know about the ketogenic diet to get you started. There are some people that may tell you different, but you get the basic concept. The ketogenic diet and instant pot certainly have a lot in common. They can be used together to create healthy dishes that are fast to prepare and tasty, and will improve your life.

The keto diet asks that you avoid greasy foods, so this is something that the instant pot can help you to do, by softening up foods using pressure and heat. With this being said let us take a look into Chapter 2 to find out a bit more about the instant pot and how it can help you to prepare healthy ketogenic meals!

Chapter 2. Everything About The Instant Pot

What is an Instant Pot?

The Instant Pot is a wonderful kitchen aide, it is a multi-cooker which was designed to prepare various meals quickly and deliciously. Using an Instant Pot, you will be able to slow cook, pressure cook, sauté, make rice, yogurt and much more, all of these can be done just by pressing a few buttons and letting your instant pot do the rest. Most models come with an automatic shut-off button, so your food will not overcook once it is ready. There is plenty of benefits connected to the instant pot, including:

The instant pot will retain minerals and vitamins

Pressure cooking will allow you to retain more minerals and vitamins, opposed to other cooking methods such as steaming or boiling. The longer you cook your foods, the more nutrition will be lost out of your food, especially when cooking vegetables. Using the instant pot that only takes minutes to cook, it will retain most of its minerals and vitamins needed to help fuel your body.

Pressure cooking can also make foods easier to digest, such as lentils and beans. In a word, cook foods in your instant pot without worrying about upsetting your stomach.

The instant pot cooks faster

With an instant pot it uses pressure and heat to cook your foods; it will take much less time to cook foods. If for example it takes you one hour to cook chicken in a conventional oven it may only take 20 minutes or less to do the same job with your instant pot.

The instant pot is very easy to use

When you are preparing your meals using the conventional oven or stovetop you need to pay full attention to make sure you do not burn or ruin your meal. With the instant pot you just need to place the ingredients into it and allow it to do the rest. No need any cooking skills, no need to stand before it when cooking. The instant pot is also very easy to clean. All you have to do is to remove the gasket from the cover and wash it with warm water.

The instant pot does not need anything else

The only kitchen appliance you will need is the instant pot. You can prepare breakfast, lunch, dinner and dessert, all with the instant pot. In this cookbook you will have 500 easy and delicious instant pot recipes to try out!

How an Instant Pot Works(Scientific Mechanism)

The instant pot is a great kitchen appliance to help you to prepare meals through pressure cooking. With pressure cooking steam is used and sealed in the pressure cooker, it is an airtight cooking pot. If you add some water, the pressure will trap the vapor that rises from the liquid. Thus, it causes the pressure to raise within the cooker, along with the temperature of the water. With the increased temperature in both water and pressure, cooking time is accelerated.

The instant pot is easy to use, all you have to do is to add your ingredients into the pot and adjust the settings. You will learn what and how to use the various buttons on your instant pot.

Instant Pot Control Panel

Below is an explanation about the different controls and settings on the instant pot:

Manual: This is the main button on your instant pot. With this button you can manually set the pressure and cooking time.

Keep Warm/Cancel: This button will cancel any functions and will turn your instant pot off. If your cooking is completed, the instant pot will automatically enter the *keep warm* mode and will stay there for 10 hours. You can cancel the function at any time.

Pressure: When you cook in manual button, this button will adjust your settings of pressure to low, medium, or high.

Slow Cook: By pressing this button you will turn your instant pot into a slow cooker.

Timer: This is the button you would use for delayed cooking. You first would select a cooking function and make any required adjustments. Then you can adjust the timer button using the +/- buttons.

Sauté: With this button it will allow you to sauté and brown your foods. When you are cooking using this button you will have the lid off, this will enable you to stir your ingredients. You can adjust the heat from sauté by pressing the normal setting, more, or less. Normal is for regular browning, more is for stir-frying, and less is for simmering.

Meat/Stew: With this button you can set your instant pot to high pressure for 35 minutes.

Poultry: This button will automatically set your instant pot to high pressure for 15 minutes.

Steam: This button will automatically place your instant pot on high for 10 minutes.

Porridge: This button will automatically set your instant pot to high pressure for 20 minutes.

Multi-Grain: This button will automatically set your instant pot at high pressure for 40 minutes.

Bean/Chili: This button will automatically set your instant pot to high pressure for 30 minutes.

Soup: This button automatically will set your instant pot to high pressure for 30 minutes.

Yogurt: Pressing this button will allow you to make yogurt using your instant pot.

You need to know how to release pressure with a pressure cooker. With the instant pot there are two ways either through natural release or quick release. Using the natural release allows the pressure to release on it own naturally. With the quick release you turn the valve on top from the 'sealing' setting to the 'venting' setting.

Choosing a Good Instant Pot

There are diverse types of instant pots available on the market. You will have to decide which is the best one for you and your needs. One of the most popular is a 6-quart version to larger and more advanced models. Below are some options you might want to consider when choosing your instant pot:

IP-DUO60

This model of instant pot is the most popular. It offers a 7-in-1 multifunctional countertop appliance; which combines a slow cooker, pressure cooker, rice cooker, yogurt maker, steamer, sauté/browning functionality and a warmer.

IP-DUO Plus60

This model is an upgrade to the regular IP-DUO60. This upgraded version includes settings such as Egg, Cake, and Sterilize buttons. The alarm clock on this model is a blue LCD screen. The inner bowl also offers more comprehensive max/min fill lines.

IP-DUO50

This model of instant pot holds five quarts.

IP-DUO80

This model of instant pot has a capacity of eight quarts. It is more expensive than others, but the extra space might be useful.

IP-LUX60 V3

This model of instant pot has egg and cake settings on the control panel. However, it does not have poultry, yogurt or beans/chili settings, nor an option to cook on low pressure. It also does not come with some of the accessories that other models have.

IP-Smart Bluetooth

This model of instant pot holds six quarts with all the basic functions, and can connect via Bluetooth to your phone; so, you are able to program and monitor cooking from anywhere using the Instant Pot Smart Cooker App.

Choosing the right instant pot for yourself should not be too complicated. It is best to purchase new appliances not used, as they could have broken buttons and complications.

Do's and Don'ts of Instant Pot

If you are new to using an instant pot it would be a clever idea to become familiar with what you should and should not do with your instant pot. Below are some helpful tips for cooking with an instant pot:

Be aware of cooking times

Cooking times are a great indicator to give you an idea when your food should be cooked, but the actual cooking time can vary. This is largely due to different ingredients being used and done in different situations. For instance, different meats will take different amounts of time to soften up. Make sure to be mindful of your cooking by inspecting the result to make sure it is cooked through. You can test a small piece from your meal that you are preparing to see that it is cooked through before removing it from the instant pot.

Make sure and read all the instructions carefully

When you get your new instant pot, read all the instructions carefully to avoid any mishaps or damaging your instant pot.

Inspect your instant pot carefully

To keep your instant pot as a reliable appliance you need to make sure that you keep it clean. If parts on your instant pot begin to wear out then they need to be replaced by original parts, or you could run the risk of permanently damaging your instant pot.

Do not overfill your instant pot

If you fill your instant pot with too much food and liquid this could cause the venting knob to become clogged. There is a max line on the inner pot make sure that you do not go past this, so you won't overfill your instant pot.

Do not press the timer button to set the cooking time

People often mistake the 'timer' button for the button to set the cook time, and then wonder why their instant pot is not working. Make sure to check that the 'timer' button is not lit before you leave.

Make sure not to add ingredients into your instant pot without the inner pot

You do not want to pour ingredients into your instant pot without its inner pot being in place, believe me this happens a lot. This can cause damage and will be time consuming to clean.

Don't use the quick release if your instant pot is overfilled or has foamy foods in it

Inexperienced users of instant pots often get the Quick Pressure Release and Natural Pressure Release confused. If you use the Quick Release when you are cooking foamy foods, such as applesauce, beans, or grains, it could splatter everywhere. To prevent this from occurring use the natural release or release the pressure gradually.

Chapter 3. Beef Instant Pot Recipes

1. *Cabbage Beef Soup*

Cook Time: 40 minutes   ***Servings: 6***

Ingredients:

- 1 head green cabbage, chopped
- 1 lb. lean ground beef
- 1 head red cabbage, chopped
- 1 can (28-ounce) tomatoes, diced
- 1 celery stalk, chopped
- 3 cups water
- 1 teaspoon fresh ground black pepper
- 1 teaspoon salt
- 1 tablespoon fresh parsley, chopped

Directions:

First press the sauté button on your instant pot. Add in the ground beef. Sauté your beef until it is no longer pink; drain. Press the keep warm/cancel setting to stop sauté mode. Return your ground beef to your instant pot. Add in the cabbage, diced tomatoes, celery, parsley, water, salt and pepper. Stir well. Close and seal the lid. Press the meat/stew button. Cook on high pressure for 20 minutes. Once completed the instant pot will automatically switch to 'keep warm' mode. Allow it to 'keep warm' mode for 10 minutes. Use the 'quick-release' when done. Open the lid carefully. Stir the ingredients, serve and garnish with fresh parsley.

Nutritional Information per serving:

Calories: 115   Fat: 4.4g   Carbohydrates: 11g   Dietary Fiber: 3g   Protein: 11g

2. *Beef & Squash Stew*

Cook Time: 50 minutes   ***Servings: 4***

Ingredients:

- 2 lbs. butternut squash, peeled, chopped into chunks
- 1 lb. lean ground beef
- 1 (6-ounce) can sliced mushrooms
- 2 garlic cloves
- 1 red onion, diced
- 4 cups beef broth
- 2 tablespoons butter
- 1 teaspoon fresh rosemary, chopped
- 1 teaspoon black pepper
- 1 teaspoon salt
- 2 teaspoons paprika

Directions:

Press the sauté button on your instant pot. Melt the butter. Sauté the garlic and onions for 1 minute. Add the ground beef, mushrooms, and butternut squash. Sauté until the beef is no longer pink and the vegetables have softened. Press the keep warm/cancel button to stop the sauté mode. Add in beef stock, paprika, salt, black pepper and rosemary, mix well. Close and seal the lid. Press the soup button. Cook on high pressure for 30 minutes. After the 30 minutes is up your instant pot will automatically switch to the 'keep warm' mode and remain in 'keep warm' for 10 minutes. Use the 'quick-release' when done and open the lid carefully, stir ingredients and serve.

Nutritional Information per serving:

Calories: 245   Fat: 17g   Protein: 25g   Carbohydrates: 5g   Dietary Fiber: 8g

3. Beef & Mixed Vegetable Stew

Cook Time: *45 minutes*   **Servings:** *4*

Ingredients:

- 4 zucchinis, chopped
- 1 ½ lbs. stewing beef chunks
- 4 cups vegetable broth
- 2 cups frozen peas
- 2 carrots, chopped
- 1 tablespoon coconut oil
- ½ cup ghee
- 4 cloves garlic, minced
- 1 red onion, chopped
- 2 tomatoes, chopped
- 1 tablespoon ginger
- 2 tablespoons cumin
- Salt and pepper to taste

Directions:

Press the sauté button on instant pot. Heat your coconut oil. Add onions and garlic and sweat for 1 minute. Add in your stewing beef and brown all sides. Add the zucchini, peas and carrots. Press the keep warm/cancel setting to stop the sauté mode. Add your ghee and stir well. Now add the vegetable stock, tomatoes, ginger, cumin, salt and pepper. Stir well. Close and seal lid of pot and press the meat/stew button. Cook for 35 minutes. When your instant pot timer beeps, quick-release or naturally release pressure. Open the pot lid carefully. Stir and spoon into serving bowls.

Nutritional Information per serving:

Calories: 200   Protein: 31g   Fat: 40g   Carbohydrates: 13g   Dietary Fiber: 4g

4. Baby Back Beef Ribs

Cook Time: *45 minutes*   **Servings:** *4*

Ingredients:

- 1 rack of baby back beef ribs
- 2 cups beef broth
- 2 tablespoons granulated Splenda
- 2 tablespoons soy sauce
- 2 tablespoons coconut oil
- 4 garlic cloves, minced
- 3 tablespoons ginger, grated
- 1 teaspoon onion powder
- 1 teaspoon cayenne pepper
- 1 teaspoon low-carb brown sugar
- 1 teaspoon ground mustard
- 1 tablespoon paprika
- 1 tablespoon chili powder
- Salt and pepper to taste

Directions:

In a small bowl mix together chili powder, ginger, ground mustard, paprika, cayenne pepper, onion powder, salt and pepper and stir well. Add in brown sugar and Splenda. Rinse your ribs, you will want the ribs to be a bit damp, so the seasoning will cling to them. Rub seasoning mix on both sides of ribs. Place the ribs on a flat baking sheet. Preheat your oven to broil. Place the baking sheet under the broiler for 5 minutes per side. Press the sauté mode on your instant pot. Heat the coconut oil. Add ginger and garlic. Cook for 1 minute.

Add soy sauce and beef broth. Boil for 15 seconds. Stir well. Press keep warm/cancel setting to end the sauté mode. Slice the rack of ribs up into chunks of 4-5 ribs and place them into your instant pot. Close and seal the lid and press manual button. Cook on high-pressure for 35 minutes. When done release the pressure quickly or naturally. Open lid carefully and serve.

Nutritional Information per serving:
Calories: 500   Fat: 40g   Carbohydrates: 1.5g   Dietary Fiber: 0.9g   Protein: 55g

---

5. *Instant Pot Keto Brisket*
Cook Time: 50 minutes   ***Servings: 5***
Ingredients:

- 2 lbs. of beef brisket
- 2 tablespoons coconut oil
- 2 shallots, thinly sliced
- 3 tablespoons tomato paste
- 1 tablespoon dry mustard

- 2 tablespoons Worcestershire sauce
- 2 tablespoons soy sauce
- 8-ounces low-carb beer
- Salt and pepper to taste

Directions:
Add all the ingredients to a large Ziploc bag and massage the ingredients. Allow them to marinate for 2 hours. When ready to cook, transfer the ingredients into your instant pot. Close the lid and press the manual setting. Cook on high-pressure for 40 minutes. Once done, quick-release or naturally release the pressure. Open the instant pot lid carefully. Press the sauté mode. Cook until all the liquids evaporate. Remove the brisket. Let rest for 15 minutes before slicing. Serve and enjoy!

Nutritional Information per serving:
Calories: 400   Fat: 20g   Carbohydrates: 3.5g   Dietary Fiber: 0.5g   Protein: 45g

---

6. *Keto Thai Beef*
Cook Time: 30 minutes   ***Servings: 6***
Ingredients:

- 1 lb. of beef, cut into strips
- 2 tablespoons coconut oil
- 4 garlic cloves, minced
- 2 teaspoons ginger, grated
- 2 cups beef broth
- Zest and juice of 1 lemon

- 1 red bell pepper, chopped
- 1 green bell pepper, chopped
- 1 tablespoon coconut amino
- 1 cup roasted pecans
- Salt and pepper to taste

Directions:
Press the sauté button on your instant pot. Heat the coconut oil. Sauté ginger and garlic for 1 minute. Add in the beef strips. Sear them for 2 minutes per side. Add bell peppers, salt and pepper. Continue to cook until meat is no longer pink. Add the coconut amino, zest and juice of lemon, pecans, and beef broth. Stir well. Close and seal lid. Press the manual setting and cook on high-pressure for 15 minutes. When done, naturally release the pressure. Open lid carefully and let sit for 10 minutes. Serve.

Nutritional Information per serving:
Calories: 225   Fat: 25g   Dietary Fiber: 1g   Carbohydrates: 10g   Protein: 20g

7. Keto Beef & Tomato Stuffed Squash

Cook Time: 30 minutes **Servings: 4**

Ingredients:

- 1 lb. of beef chopped into chunks
- 1 yellow bell pepper
- 1 green bell pepper
- 2 tablespoons ghee, melted
- 2 tablespoons coconut oil
- 1 lb. butternut squash, peeled and chopped
- 2 (14-ounce) cans of diced tomatoes
- 4 garlic cloves, minced
- 1 teaspoon cayenne pepper
- 2 tablespoons fresh parsley, chopped
- 1 tablespoon fresh rosemary, chopped
- 1 tablespoon fresh thyme, chopped
- 1 yellow or red onion, chopped
- Salt and pepper to taste

Directions:

Press sauté button on your instant pot. Heat the coconut oil. Add the onion and garlic and sweat for 2 minutes. Add the beef chunks, bell peppers, and butternut squash. Sauté until the meat is no longer pink and veggies have softened. Press keep warm/cancel to end the sauté mode. Add in the melted ghee, tomatoes, parsley, rosemary, cayenne, salt and pepper. Stir well. Close the lid and seal. Press the manual button and cook on high-pressure for 20 minutes. Quick-release the pressure when done and open lid carefully. Serve.

Nutritional Information per serving:

Calories: 250   Fat: 17g   Dietary Fiber: 2g   Carbohydrates: 4g   Protein: 10g

---

8. Keto Meatloaf

Cook Time: 35 minutes **Servings: 4**

Ingredients:

- 3 lbs. lean ground beef
- 4 garlic cloves, minced
- 1 yellow onion, chopped
- 1 cup mushrooms, chopped
- 3 large eggs
- ¼ cup parsley, fresh, chopped
- ¼ cup mozzarella cheese, grated
- ¼ cup parmesan cheese, grated
- ½ cup almond flour
- 2 cups water
- 2 tablespoons coconut oil
- 2 tablespoons sugar-free ketchup
- Salt and pepper to taste

Instructions:

Cover trivet with aluminum foil. In a large bowl, add ingredients (excluding the water) until well combined. Form into a meatloaf. Pour water in your instant pot. Place trivet inside. Place the meatloaf on trivet. Close and seal lid. Press manual button and cook on high-pressure for 25 minutes. When done, natural release the pressure. Allow meatloaf to rest for 5 minutes before slicing. Serve.

Nutritional Information per serving:

Calories: 250   Fat: 15g   Dietary Fiber: 3g   Carbohydrates: 5g   Protein: 25g

9. Ginger Beef & Kale

Cook Time: 35 minutes   **Servings: 4**

Ingredients:

- 1 lb. beef cut into chunks
- 1 bunch of kale, stemmed, chopped
- 2 tablespoons coconut oil
- 2 tablespoons ginger, fresh, grated
- 4 garlic cloves, minced
- 1 red onion, chopped
- 2 cups beef broth
- 1 teaspoon paprika
- ½ lb. mushrooms, sliced
- Salt and pepper to taste
- Sesame seeds for garnish
- 2 spring onions, chopped, for garnish

Directions:

Press sauté button on your instant pot. Heat your coconut oil. Add in the onions and garlic and sweat for 1 minute. Add the beef chunks and sauté until the meat is no longer pink. Press the keep warm/cancel setting to end the sauté mode. Add in the remaining ingredients. Stir well. Close and seal the lid. Press manual button and cook at high-pressure for 25 minutes. When the timer beeps, quick-release or naturally release pressure. Open the lid and stir ingredients. Divide into serving plates, garnish with sesame seeds and chopped spring onion. Serve.

Nutritional Information per serving:

Calories: 325   Fat: 25g   Carbohydrates: 10g   Dietary Fiber: 2.5g   Protein: 30g

10. Salisbury Steak

Cook Time: 35 minutes   **Servings: 4**

Ingredients:

- 2 lbs. lean ground beef
- 1 tablespoon coconut oil
- ½ yellow onion, diced
- 1 tablespoon Worcestershire sauce
- ¼ cup beef broth
- ¼ cup coconut flour
- 1 egg
- 1 tablespoon bread crumbs
- 2 garlic cloves, minced
- 1 tablespoon parsley, fresh, chopped
- Salt and pepper to taste

Gravy Ingredients:

- 2 cups mushrooms, sliced
- 2 tablespoons ghee, melted
- 1 onion, sliced
- 2 tablespoons parsley, fresh, chopped
- ¼ cup sour cream
- 1 tablespoon tomato paste
- 1 teaspoon Worcestershire sauce
- Salt and pepper to taste

Directions:

In a large mixing bowl, steak ingredients, except coconut oil. Shape into round patties, ¼ inch thick. Set aside. Press your sauté button on your instant pot. Heat the coconut oil. Cook the patties 2 minutes per side, until they are golden brown. Remove the patties and set aside. Heat the ghee and add gravy ingredients. Stir well. Press the keep warm/cancel button to end sauté mode. Return patties to your instant pot. Close and seal the lid. Press manual switch and cook at high-pressure for 25 minutes. When done quick-release pressure. Open lid carefully. Serve.

Nutritional Information per serving:
Calories: 425   Fat: 35g   Carbohydrates: 5g   Protein: 32g   Dietary Fiber: 1g

---

11. *Keto Corned Beef*
Cook Time: 60 minutes
Servings: 6
Ingredients:

- 4 lbs. beef brisket
- 2 oranges, sliced
- 2 garlic cloves, minced
- 3 bay leaves
- 1 tablespoon dried dill
- 11 ounces celery, sliced thin
- 2 yellow onions, sliced thin
- 4 cinnamon sticks, cut in half
- 17 ounces of water
- Salt and pepper to taste

Directions:
Place your beef in a bowl, and cover with some water, set aside to soak for a few hours, drain and transfer to your instant pot. Add in orange slices, celery, bay leaves, onions, garlic, dill, cinnamon, salt and pepper. Stir and cover instant pot and cook on the meat/stew setting for 50 minutes. Release using quick-release or natural release of pressure, set the beef aside for 5 minutes. Transfer meat to cutting board, slice and place onto serving plates. Drizzle the juice and vegetables from instant pot over the beef. Serve.

Nutritional Information per serving:
Calories: 251   Fat: 5.14g   Fiber: 1g   Carbs: 1.1g   Protein: 17g

---

12. *Beef Bourguignon*
Cook Time: 30 minutes
Servings: 6
Ingredients:

- 10 lbs. round steak, cut into small cubes
- 2 tablespoons white flour
- 8 ounces mushrooms, cut into quarters
- 3 bacon slices, chopped
- 1 cup dry red wine
- ½ cup beef stock
- 2 carrots, peeled and sliced
- 12 pearl onions
- 2 garlic cloves, minced
- ¼ teaspoon basil, dried
- Salt and pepper to taste

Directions:
Set the instant pot on sauté mode, add the bacon, and brown it for two minutes. Add the beef pieces, stir and brown for 5 minutes. Add the flour and stir. Add wine, basil, garlic, onions, salt and pepper, cover and cook on the meat/stew setting for 20 minutes. Release the pressure, naturally, uncover the instant pot and add in the mushrooms and carrots. Cover the instant pot again and cook on manual setting for 5 minutes. Release the pressure again naturally, divide the beef bourguignon among serving plates. Serve.

Nutritional Information per serving:
Calories: 442   Fat: 17.2g   Fiber: 3g   Carbs: 3.6g   Protein: 39g

13. Beef Curry
Cook Time: 20 minutes
Servings: 4
Ingredients:

- 2 lbs. beef steak, cubed
- 3 potatoes, diced
- 2 tablespoons virgin olive oil
- 1 tablespoon Dijon mustard
- 2 garlic cloves, minced
- 2 yellow onions, chopped
- 2 ½ tablespoons curry powder
- 10 ounces canned coconut milk
- 2 tablespoons tomato sauce
- Salt and pepper to taste

Directions:

Set your instant pot to sauté mode, add oil, and heat. Add the garlic and onions and cook for 4 minutes. Add the potatoes and mustard, stir, cook for 1 minute. Add the beef and brown on all sides. Add the curry powder, salt and pepper and cook for 2 minutes. Add the coconut milk and tomato sauce, stir and cover your instant pot. Cook on the meat/stew setting for 10 minutes. Release the pressure with quick-release and then uncover pot. Divide the curry onto serving plates. Serve.

Nutritional Information per serving:

Calories: 434   Fat: 25g   Fiber: 2.9g   Carbs: 4g   Protein: 27.5g

14. Beef Stroganoff
Cook Time: 25 minutes
Servings: 4
Ingredients:

- 10 lbs. beef, cut into small cubes
- 2 ½ tablespoons almond flour
- 2 garlic cloves, minced
- 2 ½ tablespoons olive oil
- 4 ounces mushrooms, sliced
- 1 ½ tablespoon tomato paste
- 3 tablespoons Worcestershire sauce
- 13 ounces beef stock
- 8 ounces sour cream
- Egg noodles, already cooked, for serving
- Salt and pepper to taste

Directions:

Put all the beef, flour, salt and pepper in a bowl and toss to coat. Set your instant pot on sauté mode, add olive oil, and heat. Add in the meat and brown on all sides. Add the garlic, mushrooms, onion, Worcestershire sauce, stock and tomato paste and mix well. Cover instant pot and cook on the meat/stew setting for 20 minutes. Use quick-release to release the pressure. Remove the top of pot and add in the sour cream, salt and pepper. Divide among serving plates. Serve.

Nutritional Information per serving:

Calories: 335   Fat: 18.4g   Fiber: 1.3g   Carbs: 2.5g   Protein: 20.1g

15. Keto Beef Chili
Cook Time: 40 minutes
Servings: 6
Ingredients:

- 1 ½ lbs. ground beef
- 17 ounces beef stock
- 16 ounces mixed beans, soaked overnight and drained
- 1 sweet onion, chopped
- 28 ounces canned diced tomatoes
- 6 garlic cloves, chopped
- 1 teaspoon chili powder
- 1 bay leaf
- 3 tablespoons chili powder
- 4 carrots, chopped
- 2 tablespoons olive oil
- 7 jalapeno peppers, diced

Directions:
Set your instant pot on sauté mode and add half of the olive oil and heat it up. Add in the beef and brown for 8 minutes, then transfer to a bowl. Add the rest of the oil to the instant pot and heat up. Add in the jalapenos, onion, carrots and garlic, stir and sauté for 4 minutes. Add tomatoes and stir. Add beans, stock, chili powder, bay leaf, beef, salt and pepper. Cover and cook on the bean/chilli setting for 25 minutes. Release the pressure naturally, uncover your instant pot, stir chili and transfer into serving bowls. Serve.

Nutritional Information per serving:
Calories: 272   Fat: 15g   Fiber: 1g   Carbs: 3.2g   Protein: 25g

16. Keto Chili Con Carne
Cook Time: 30 minutes
Servings: 4
Ingredients:

- 1 lb. of ground beef
- 4 tablespoons coconut oil
- 1 yellow onion, chopped
- 2 garlic cloves, minced
- 4 ounces kidney beans, soaked overnight and drained
- 8 ounces tomatoes, canned, diced
- 1 tablespoon chili powder
- ½ teaspoon cumin
- 5 ounces water
- 1 teaspoon tomato paste

Directions:
Set your instant pot to sauté mode, add 1 tablespoon coconut oil and heat it up. Add in the meat and brown for a few minutes then transfer to a bowl. Add the rest of the coconut oil to the instant pot and heat it up. Add in the garlic, and onion and cook for 3 minutes. Return the beef to pot, beans, tomato paste, chili powder, tomatoes, cumin, salt, pepper and water. Cover pot and cook on the bean/chili setting for 18 minutes. Release the pressure naturally. Uncover the instant pot and divide the chili into serving bowls. Serve.

Nutritional Information per serving:
Calories: 256   Fat: 8g   Fiber: 1g   Carbs: 2.2g   Protein: 35g

17. Beef Pot Roast

Cook Time: 1 hour

Servings: 6

Ingredients:

- 3 lbs. beef roast
- 17 ounces beef stock
- 3 ounces red wine
- 1 yellow onion, chopped
- 4 garlic cloves, minced
- 3 carrots, chopped
- 5 potatoes, chopped
- ½ teaspoon smoked paprika
- Salt and pepper to taste

Directions:

In a bowl mix the salt, pepper and paprika and rub on beef and place it into the instant pot. Add the garlic, stock, wine, onion, and toss to coat. Cover the instant pot and cook on meat/stew setting for 50 minutes. Release the pressure naturally. Uncover the instant pot and add in the potatoes and carrots and cover it again. Cook on the steam setting for 10 minutes. Release the pressure naturally again, uncover and transfer the roast to a serving platter. Drizzle roast with cooking juices and serve with the veggies on the side.

Nutritional Information per serving:

Calories: 290   Fat: 20g   Fiber: 1g   Carbs: 2g   Protein: 35g

18. Beef & Vegetables

Cook Time: 30 minutes

Servings: 4

Ingredients:

- 1 ½ lbs. beef chuck roast, cubed
- 2 tablespoons of coconut oil
- 4 tablespoons almond flour
- 1 yellow onion, chopped
- 2 cups water
- 2 garlic cloves, minced
- 2 tablespoons red wine
- ½ bunch parsley, chopped
- 4 potatoes, chopped
- 2 carrots, chopped
- 2 celery stalks, chopped
- ½ teaspoon thyme, dried
- 2 cups beef stock
- Salt and pepper to taste

Directions:

Mix the salt and pepper with half of almond flour and season the beef with it. Set the instant pot on sauté mode, add the coconut oil and heat it up. Add the beef and brown it for 2 minutes. Once meat is browned transfer to bowl. Add the onion to the instant pot and cook for 3 minutes. Add the garlic, stir and cook for 1 minute. Add the wine, stir and cook for 15 seconds. Add the rest of the almond flour and stir for 2 minutes.

Return the meat to the instant pot, add water, thyme, stock and cover and cook on meat/stew setting for 12 minutes. Release the pressure naturally. Remove the lid of instant pot and add potatoes and carrots into pot. Cover pot and cook on steam setting for 5 minutes. Release the pressure naturally. Uncover the instant pot, divide among serving plates, serve with parsley sprinkled on top.

Nutritional Information per serving:

Calories: 221   Fat: 5.3g   Fiber: 1g   Carbs: 2.2g   Protein: 32.7g

19. Veal with Mushrooms

Cook Time: 35 minutes   **Servings: 4**

Ingredients:

- 3.5 ounces button mushrooms, sliced
- 3.5 ounces shiitake mushrooms, sliced
- 9 ounces beef stock
- 16 ounces shallots, chopped
- 17 ounces potatoes, chopped
- 2 lbs. veal shoulder, cut into medium chunks
- 3 ½ tablespoons coconut oil
- 1/8 teaspoon thyme, dried
- 1 teaspoon sage, dried
- 2 tablespoons chives, chopped
- 2 garlic cloves, minced
- 1 tablespoon almond flour
- 2 ounces white wine
- Salt and pepper to taste

Directions:

Set your instant pot to sautė mode and add 1 1/2tablespoons of coconut oil and heat it up. Add the veal, season with salt and pepper, brown for 5 minutes and transfer to bowl. Add the rest of coconut oil into instant pot and heat it up. Add the mushrooms and stir and cook for 3 minutes. Add the garlic and cook for 1 minute, transfer to bowl.

Add the almond flour and wine to the instant pot and cook for 1 minute. Add the stock, thyme and sage to instant pot and return the meat to pot. Stir, cover and cook on the meat/stew setting for 20 minutes. Release the pressure naturally. Uncover the pot, return the garlic and mushrooms, add the potatoes, shallots stir and cover. Cook on the manual setting for 4 minutes. Release the pressure again and uncover the pot, add salt and pepper, chives and stir. Divide among serving bowls. Serve.

Nutritional Information per serving:

Calories: 395   Fat: 18g   Fiber: 1.4g   Carbs: 7.1g   Protein: 47.8g

20. Beef & Kale Casserole

Cook Time: 20 minutes   **Servings: 4**

Ingredients:

- 2 cups of kale, fresh, chopped
- 1 lb. ground beef
- 13 ounces mozzarella cheese, shredded
- 16 ounces tomato puree
- 1 celery stalk
- 1 carrot, chopped
- 1 yellow onion, chopped
- 2 tablespoons butter
- 1 tablespoons red wine
- Salt and pepper to taste

Directions:

Set your instant pot on sautė mode, add the butter and melt it. Add the onion, carrot, stir and cook for 5 minutes. Add the beef, salt, pepper and cook for 10 minutes. Add the wine and stir and cook for 1 minute. Add the kale, tomato puree, cover with water and stir set on manual setting for 6 minutes. Release the pressure naturally. Uncover the pot and add the cheese and stir. Divide into serving bowls. Serve.

Nutritional Information per serving:

Calories: 182   Fat: 11g   Fiber: 1.4g   Carbs: 3.1g   Protein: 22g

21. Korean Beef
Cook Time: 25 minutes   **Servings: 6**
Ingredients:

- 1 cup beef stock
- ¼ cup soybean paste
- 2 lbs. beefsteak, cut into strips
- 1 yellow onion, sliced thin
- 1-ounce shiitake mushroom caps, cut into quarters
- 1 zucchini, cubed
- ¼ teaspoon red pepper flakes
- 1 scallion, chopped
- 1 chili pepper, sliced
- 12 ounces extra firm tofu, cubed
- Salt and pepper to taste

Directions:
Set the instant pot on sauté mode and add the stock and soybean paste, stir and simmer for 2 minutes. Add the beef, pepper flakes, salt and pepper. Cover the instant pot and cook on the meat/stew setting for 15 minutes. Release the pressure naturally. Add the zucchini, onion, tofu, and mushrooms, stir and bring to a boil. Cover the instant pot and cook on manual setting for 4 minutes. Release the pressure naturally again, uncover the instant pot, add more salt and pepper, add the chili pepper and scallion. Stir. Divide into serving bowls. Serve.
Nutritional Information per serving:
Calories: 310   Fat: 19.3g   Fiber: 0.2g   Carbs: 8.4g   Protein: 35.3g

22. Beef & Broccoli
Cook Time: 10 minutes   **Servings: 4**
Ingredients:

- 3 lbs. beef chuck roast, cut into thin strips
- 1 tablespoon peanut oil
- 2 tablespoons almond flour

For the marinade:

- 1 tablespoon sesame oil
- 2 tablespoons fish sauce
- 1 cup soy sauce
- 5 garlic cloves, minced
- 2 teaspoons toasted sesame oil
- 1 lb. broccoli florets
- 1 yellow onion, chopped
- ½ cup beef stock

- 3 red peppers, crushed, dried
- ½ teaspoon Chinese five spice powder
- Toasted sesame seeds for serving

Directions:
Mix the soy sauce, with the fish sauce and 1 tablespoon of sesame oil in a bowl. Add in garlic and five spice powder along with crushed red peppers and stir well. Add the beef strips and toss to coat. Set the instant pot to sauté mode, adding peanut oil and heat it up. Add the onions and cook for 4 minutes. Add the beef and marinade and cook for 2 minutes. Add the stock and stir, cover the instant pot. Cook on the meat/stew setting in 5 minutes. Release the pressure naturally for 10 minutes.
Uncover the instant pot and add the almond flour with ¼ cup liquid from the instant pot, add the broccoli to the steamer basket, cover the instant pot again and cook for 3 minutes

on manual mode. Release the pressure and uncover the instant pot and divide the beef into serving bowls add the broccoli on top and drizzle with toasted sesame seeds. Serve.

Nutritional Information per serving:

Calories: 338 Fat: 18g Fiber: 5g Carbs: 5g Protein: 40g

---

23. Beef and Cabbage

Cook Time: 1 hour and 20 minutes   **Servings: 6**

Ingredients:

- 2 ½ lbs. beef brisket
- 6 potatoes, cut into quarters
- 1 cabbage head, cut into wedges
- 4 carrots, peeled and chopped
- 3 cloves garlic, peeled, chopped
- 2 bay leaves
- 4 cups water
- 1 turnip cut into quarters
- Horseradish sauce, for serving
- Salt and pepper to taste

Directions:

Add the beef brisket and water into your instant pot, add garlic, bay leaves, salt and pepper, cover the instant pot. Set on the meat/stew setting for 1 hour and 15 minutes. Release the pressure with quick-release. Add to instant pot carrots, potatoes, cabbage, and turnip, stir and cover. Cook on the manual setting for 6 minutes. Release the pressure naturally, and uncover your instant pot. Divide among serving plates. Serve with horseradish sauce on top.

Nutritional Information per serving:

Calories: 340 Fat: 24g Fiber: 1g Carbs: 4g Protein: 46g

---

24. Instant Pot Beef Cabbage Rolls

Cook Time: 38 minutes   **Servings: 6**

Ingredients:

- 2 lbs. lean ground beef
- ½ teaspoon, freshly ground black pepper
- 4 cloves garlic, minced, finely
- 1 cup green onion

For the sauce:

- 1 cup onion, finely chopped
- 2 tablespoons butter
- 3 cloves of garlic, finely minced
- Chopped, fresh parsley for garnish
- 2 tablespoons cold water
- 1 tablespoon cornstarch
- 4 dashes Worcestershire sauce
- ½ teaspoon freshly ground black pepper

- 1 large egg
- 1 large head of cabbage
- 1 cup brown rice
- 1 teaspoon sea salt

- 1 teaspoon onion powder
- ½ teaspoon garlic powder
- ¼ cup white vinegar
- 2 teaspoons low-sodium instant beef bouillon
- 1 (8-ounce can) tomato sauce
- 2 (14-ounce cans) tomatoes, diced with their juice

Directions:

Cook the brown rice according to package directions. Fluff with fork and set aside. Fill a deep large pot half full of water, and bring to a boil over high heat. Remove the core from the cabbage, and place the cabbage core side down into the pot of water. Cover and allow the head of cabbage to boil for 10 minutes. Keep checking and removing the outer leaves as they soften on the cabbage, removing them to a plate to cool. Once you have removed all the large leaves to make rolls, cook the smaller leaves until they are crisp-tender. When done remove them from heat and coarsely chop them and set aside.

For your sauce take a large saucepan and melt the butter in it, add the onion, and cook over medium heat for 2 minutes, add the garlic and stir for another minute. Add in the tomatoes, bouillon, vinegar, garlic powder, Worcestershire sauce, onion powder, salt and pepper, mix well. Remove from heat and stir in some of the chopped cabbage and set aside.

For your cabbage roll filling add to a large bowl, beaten egg, onion, cooked rice, garlic, salt, pepper, ground beef and mix with your hands until ingredients are well combined.

Take a cabbage leaf and lay it flat on a work surface with the stem end facing you. Take to tablespoonfuls of filling and place it at the bottom of the cabbage leaf. Fold in the sides of the leaf and roll away from you. Repeat this with the remaining cabbage leaves and filling, on average you should get about 15 rolls.

Place a layer of sauce in your instant pot then a layer of cabbage rolls, repeat this, layer, do not fill too much, you might have to do two batches. Secure the lid so that it is sealed and set to the Meat/Stew setting for 20 minutes. When the cooking is completed, release the pressure naturally for 15 minutes, then use quick-release to get rid of any remaining steam. Remove cabbage rolls to a platter. Set instant pot to sauté mode and bring sauce to a boil. In small bowl whisk the cornstarch and cold water, then add into sauce to thicken. Divide rolls into serving bowls, pour sauce over rolls. Serve hot!

Nutritional Information per serving:
Calories: 389   Fat: 25g   Fiber: 1g   Carbs: 2.3g   Protein: 37g

25. Beef & Mushroom Soup

Cook Time: 25 minutes   **Servings: 4**

Ingredients:

- 1 ½ lbs. steak, thinly sliced
- 32 ounces beef stock
- 10 ounces Cremini mushrooms, thinly sliced
- 3 tablespoons butter
- 3 tablespoons garlic, minced
- 1 medium onion, diced
- 1 cup heavy cream
- 1 cup sour cream

- 2 tablespoons beef bouillon granules
- 2 tablespoons Dijon mustard
- 2 tablespoons Italian parsley, chopped
- 1 ½ teaspoons onion powder
- 1 ½ teaspoons garlic powder
- 1 teaspoon Oregano, dried
- 1 teaspoon sea salt
- Black pepper to taste

Directions:
Set your instant pot onto sauté mode and add the butter and heat. Add in the onions and garlic. Add in the beef strips, mushrooms and beef stock. Sauté for a few minutes or until

beef is no longer pink. Press the keep warm/cancel button to stop sauté mode. Add in rest of ingredients and press the meat/stew button on instant and set for 20 minutes. Release pressure naturally. Remove lid and divide into serving bowls. Serve.

Nutritional Information per serving:
Calories: 310   Fat: 18.4g   Fiber: 1.3g   Carbs: 2.5g   Protein: 30.1g

26. *Spicy Beef & Cashew Curry*

Cook Time: 20 minutes   ***Servings: 4***

Ingredients:

- 2lbs chuck roast
- 6 tablespoons coconut milk
- 2 tablespoons Thai fish sauce
- 2 red chilis, fresh, chopped
- 1 tablespoon onion flakes
- 1 tablespoon cumin, ground
- 5 cardamom pods, cracked
- 3 tablespoons red curry paste

- 2 cups water
- 1 tablespoon coriander, ground
- 1 tablespoon ginger, ground
- ¼ cup cashews, roughly chopped, for garnish when serving
- ¼ cup cilantro, fresh, chopped, top when serving
- 2 tablespoons coconut oil

Directions:
Set your instant pot on sauté mode and add coconut oil and heat. Add in the beef and brown on all sides for a few minutes. Press the keep warm/cancel button to cancel sauté mode once meat is browned. Set instant pot to meat/stew setting for 20 minutes. Add remaining ingredients to instant pot except the cashews and cilantro. Release pressure naturally. Open the lid and divide into serving dishes. Serve.

Nutritional Information per serving:
Calories: 374   Fat: 20g   Fiber: 2.6g   Carbs: 4g   Protein: 35.5g

27. *BBQ Pot Roast with Garlic Sauce*

Cook Time: 1 hour   ***Servings: 4***

Ingredients:

- 4 lbs. chuck shoulder roast
- 5 teaspoons garlic, minced
- 1 yellow onion, chopped
- 2 tablespoons Worcestershire sauce
- 3 tablespoons butter

- 4 tablespoons vinegar
- 1 tablespoon mustard
- 1 teaspoon liquid smoke
- Salt and pepper to taste

Directions:
Rub the roast with salt and pepper. Set instant pot to sauté and add butter, then add the roast and brown meat on all sides. Press keep warm/cancel button to cancel the sauté mode. Add all other ingredients into the instant pot and set on meat/stew setting for 1 hour. Release the pressure naturally. Open the lid of pot and stir. Divide into serving dishes. Serve with choice of veggies.

Nutritional Information per serving:
Calories: 270   Fat: 20g   Fiber: 1g   Carbs: 2g   Protein: 23g

28. Cheesesteak Casserole

Cook Time: 1 hour　　　　　　　　　　**Servings: 6**

Ingredients:

- 2 lbs cube steak, cut into strips
- 1 red pepper, cut into strips
- 1 green pepper, cut into strips
- ½ lb. mushroom, sliced
- ¼ lb. pepperoni, thinly sliced
- 8 ounces provolone cheese, thinly sliced
- 1 tablespoon coconut oil
- 1 onion, thinly sliced
- Salt and pepper to taste

Directions:

Set your instant pot to sauté mode, and add in the coconut oil. Add the mushrooms and steak and saute until meat is no longer pink. Add in remaining ingredients except the cheese, and press the keep warm/cancel button to cancel sauté mode. Set your instant pot to the meat/stew setting for 50 minutes. Release pressure naturally. Remove the lid and stir. Divide into serving dishes. Top each dish with cheese, allow cheese to melt and then serve.

Nutritional Information per serving:

Calories: 296　Fat: 18.4g　Fiber: 1.3g　Carbs: 2.5g　Protein: 30.1g

29. Cabbage Stew and Beef Shank

Cook Time: 50 minutes　　　　　　　**Servings: 4**

Ingredients:

- 2 center-cut beef shanks
- 4 cloves garlic, minced
- ½ lb. baby carrots
- 2 medium onions, chopped
- 1 small cabbage, cut into wedges
- 15-ounce can tomato, diced, drained
- 1 cup beef stock
- Salt and pepper to taste
- 2 tablespoons coconut oil

Directions:

Set your instant pot to sauté mode, and add in coconut oil. Add in the beef shanks and sauté until the meat is no longer pink. Press the keep warm/cancel button to stop sauté mode. Open lid of instant pot and add rest of ingredients. Set on meat/stew setting for 50 minutes. Release pressure naturally. Open lid and stir. Remove the meat and shred with fork. Divide into serving dishes. Serve.

Nutritional Information per serving:

Calories: 310　Fat: 22g　Fiber: 1g　Carbs: 4g　Protein: 42g

30. Shredded Beef with Avocado Salsa

Cook Time: 1 hour and 10 minutes   **Servings: 6**

Ingredients:

- 2 lbs. beef chuck roast, cut into strips
- 1 tablespoon taco seasoning

Cabbage Slaw & Dressing Ingredients:

- ½ a small head of cabbage
- 1 small green cabbage
- ½ cup thinly sliced green onion

Avocado Salsa Ingredients:

- 2 large avocados, diced
- 1 tablespoon lime juice, fresh squeezed

- 2 tablespoons coconut oil
- 2 cans diced green chilies with juice

- 2 teaspoons green tabasco sauce
- 6 tablespoons mayo
- 4 teaspoons lime juice, fresh squeezed

- 1 medium Poblano pepper, diced very small
- 1 tablespoon extra-virgin olive oil
- 1 cup cilantro, freshly chopped

Directions:

Remove all excess fat from the meat and cut into strips. Season the meat strips with taco seasoning. Set your instant pot to sauté mode. Add in coconut oil and meat, sauté until meat is no longer pink and browned on all sides. Press the keep warm/cancel button to stop sauté once the meat is browned. Set to meat/stew setting for 1 hour. Release the pressure naturally. Remove the meat from instant pot and shred on chopping board with a fork. Place shredded meat back into your instant pot and replace the lid and keep on the keep warm/cancel setting. Slice the cabbage and the green onions to tiny strips using a slicer. Make the dressing by whisking the green Tabasco, mayo, and lime juice together. Mix the strips of cabbage and onions with the dressing. Slice the avocados and mix with lime juice. Chop cilantro and Poblano pepper very finely, and mix with the avocado. Pour in olive oil and mix. Place slaw in serving bowls. Top with beef and avocado salsa. Serve.

Nutritional Information per serving:

Calories: 296   Fat: 21g   Fiber: 1g   Carbs: 8g   Protein: 33g

31. Cheeseburger Soup

Cook Time: 25 minutes   **Servings: 4**

Ingredients:

- 1 lb lean ground beef
- 4 cups beef broth low sodium
- 1 teaspoon Worcestershire sauce
- 2 teaspoons parsley, fresh chopped
- ½ red bell pepper
- 2 tomatoes, chopped

- 8 ounces tomato paste
- ½ cup onions, chopped
- 1 teaspoon garlic powder
- ½ cup cheese
- Salt and pepper to taste
- 2 tablespoons coconut oil

Directions:

Set your instant pot to sauté mode. Add the coconut oil. Add in the ground beef and sauté until the meat is no longer pink and is browned. Press the keep warm/cancel button to stop sauté mode. Set the instant pot to meat/stew setting for 20 minutes. Add the rest of the ingredients and stir. Close the lid. Once done release pressure naturally. Add to serving dishes. Top with cheese. Serve.

Nutritional Information per serving:
Calories: 187   Fat: 5g   Fiber: 1.4g   Carbs: 3.2g   Protein: 38g

---

32. *Beef Sirloin Lettuce Wraps*
Cook Time: 40 minutes   ***Servings: 6***
Ingredients:
- 2 lbs. sirloin roast, excess fat removed
- 1 teaspoon smoked paprika
- 1 tablespoon chili powder
- 2 cups beef broth
- 1 onion, chopped
- Salt and pepper to taste
- Lettuce leaves to use to wrap meat, as needed

Directions:
Add all your ingredients into your instant pot. Set your instant pot on the meat/stew setting for 40 minutes. Once done release the pressure naturally. Remove the lid and stir. Remove the meat to chopping board and shred the meat with a fork. Return the meat to the instant pot. Place lettuce leaves on serving plates then top them with meat. Serve.

Nutritional Information per serving:
Calories: 296   Fat: 20g   Fiber: 1g   Carbs: 1.4g   Protein: 37g

---

33. *Ropa Vieja*
Cook Time: 25 minutes   ***Servings: 4***
Ingredients:
- 2 lbs. flank steak, cut into strips
- 1 yellow pepper
- 1 green pepper
- 1 onion, thinly sliced
- 4 teaspoons cumin
- 4 teaspoons oregano
- 3 teaspoons garlic, minced
- 3 tablespoons tomato paste
- 1 tablespoon capers
- Sea salt to taste
- 2 tablespoons olive oil

Directions:
Add the olive oil to your instant pot and set it to sauté mode. Add in meat strips and sauté until browned. Press the keep warm/cancel button to turn off the sauté mode. Add remaining ingredients into the pot and set to meat/stew setting for 20 minutes. Release the pressure with quick-release. Remove the lid and stir ingredients. Divide into serving dishes. Serve.

Nutritional Information per serving:
Calories: 282   Fat: 20g   Fiber: 1g   Carbs: 1.4g   Protein: 39g

34. Italian-style Beef
Cook Time: 45 minutes   **Servings: 4**
Ingredients:

- 2 lbs. boneless beef brisket
- 6 cloves of garlic, minced
- 1 onion, sliced
- 1 teaspoon red pepper flakes
- ½ cup red wine
- 2 cups fat-free beef broth
- Salt and pepper to taste
- 1 tablespoon Italian seasoning

Directions:

Rub the beef with salt and pepper. Place the beef along with the rest of the ingredients into your instant pot. Set to meat/stew setting for 45 minutes. Once done release the pressure naturally. Remove the lid and stir. Remove the meat and shred with fork then place it back into the instant pot.

Nutritional Information per serving:

Calories: 274   Fat: 22g   Fiber: 1g   Carbs: 1.6g   Protein: 42g

35. Asian Shredded Beef
Cook Time: 50 minutes   **Servings: 4**
Ingredients:

- 2 lbs. beef eye of round roast
- ¼ cup rice wine vinegar
- ½ cup soy sauce
- ¼ cup brown sugar
- 2 tablespoons ketchup
- 2 tablespoons sesame seeds
- 1-inch piece of ginger, fresh, grated
- 2 teaspoons Asian chili sauce
- 6 cloves of garlic, minced
- ½ red onion, minced
- 1 jalapeno, minced

Directions:

In a bowl add the soy sauce, brown sugar, vinegar, sesame seeds, ginger, ketchup, Asian chili sauce. Whisk these ingredients, add in the onion, jalapeno, and garlic. Place the roast into the instant pot. Pour the sauce over the roast. Cook on the meat/stew setting for 50 minutes. When done release naturally. Remove the meat and shred the meat with a fork. Replace the meat back into the instant pot. Allow it to sit for 30 minutes on the keep warm setting.

Nutritional Information per serving:

Calories: 287   Fat: 22g   Fiber: 1g   Carbs: 2g   Protein: 36g

36. Instant Pot Beef Ragu with Herbs
Cook Time: 30 minutes   **Servings: 4**
Ingredients:

- 2 lbs lean chuck beef
- ½ onion, diced
- 1 rib of celery, diced
- 2 tablespoons oregano, fresh, chopped
- 2 tablespoons rosemary, fresh, minced
- 1.5 cups beef broth
- 1-14 ounce can tomatoes, diced

- 1-14 ounce can tomatoes, crushed
- 4 garlic cloves, minced
- 1 carrot, peeled, diced

Directions:

Rub the meat with salt and pepper and place it in the instant pot. Add remaining ingredients to the instant pot. Set to meat/stew setting and cook for 30 minutes. Once done then release the pressure naturally. Remove the lid and stir ingredients. Divide into serving dishes. Serve.

Nutritional Information per serving:

Calories: 292   Fat: 19g   Fiber: 2g   Carbs: 4g   Protein: 36g

37. Hot Roast Machaca

Cook Time: 45 minutes   **Servings: 4**

Ingredients:

- 2 lbs. rump roast
- 3 serrano chiles, stemmed, seeded, and minced
- 3 garlic cloves, minced
- 1 cup red bell pepper, diced
- 1 ½ cups onion, diced
- 4 tablespoons fresh lime juice
- 2 tablespoons Worcestershire sauce
- 2 tablespoons of Maggi sauce
- Salt and pepper to taste
- ½ cup beef broth
- ½ teaspoon oregano, dried
- ½ 14-ounce can diced tomatoes with juice

Directions:

Rub the meat with salt and pepper and place into your instant pot. In a bowl mix Maggi, beef broth and lime juice. Pour the mixture over the meat. Add all other ingredients into instant pot. Set to meat/stew setting for 45 minutes. Once it is done release pressure naturally. Remove the lid and stir the ingredients, remove meat shred with fork. Return meat to pot. Keep on warm setting for 20 minutes. Divide into serving dishes. Serve.

Nutritional Information per serving:

Calories: 296   Fat: 23g   Fiber: 3g   Carbs: 4g   Protein: 34g

38. Korean-style Beef Tacos

Cook Time: 55 minutes   **Servings: 6**

Ingredients:

- 2 lbs. beef roast
- ½ tablespoon Truvia
- 1/3 soy sauce
- 4 garlic cloves, minced
- 1-inch ginger root, fresh, peeled, grated
- ½ red onion, diced
- 2 jalapenos, diced
- 2 tablespoons seasoned rice wine vinegar
- 2 tablespoons sesame seeds
- Serve on flour tortillas

Directions:

In a bowl add Truvia, sesame seeds, jalapenos, ginger and mix well. Add in the rice wine vinegar and soy sauce. Add the beef into instant pot, rub garlic into meat. Pour sauce over the meat and place lid on instant pot. Set to meat/stew setting for 55 minutes. When done release the pressure naturally. Remove the meat and shred, then place back into the instant pot and allow to stay for 20 minutes on keep warm setting. Divide into serving dishes on top of flour tortillas. Serve.

Nutritional Information per serving:

Calories: 302   Fat: 23g   Fiber: 3g   Carbs: 5g   Protein: 34g

---

39. Instant Pot Beef Stew

Cook Time: 40 minutes   **Servings: 4**

Ingredients:

- 2 lbs cubed beef
- 1 tablespoon ghee
- 2 cups beef broth
- 1 red onion, sliced
- 1 carrot, peeled, chopped
- 2 celery stalks, diced
- 1 cinnamon stick
- 5 cloves
- ¼ teaspoon nutmeg
- 1-star anise
- Salt and pepper to taste
- Head of lettuce

Directions:

Set your instant pot to sauté mode, add in the ghee. Place your cubed beef into instant pot and brown on all sides. Also add onion. When you are finished with sautéing the meat and onions press the keep warm/cancel button to stop the sauté mode. Place your other ingredients into instant pot along with meat and onions. Set your instant pot to meat/stew setting for 35 minutes. Once done release pressure naturally. Stir the ingredients. Add lettuce leaves to serving dished then top with meat mixture.

Nutritional Information per serving:

Calories: 292   Fat: 21g   Fiber: 3g   Carbs: 6g   Protein: 32g

---

40. Caribbean Ginger Oxtails

Cook Time: 45 minutes   **Servings: 4**

Ingredients:

- 2 lbs. beef oxtails
- 2 carrots, diced
- 2 onions, sliced
- 4 sprigs thyme, fresh
- 1 teaspoon fish sauce
- 3 tablespoons tomato paste
- 2 cups beef stock
- 1 jalapeno pepper, minced
- 4 garlic cloves, minced
- 1-inch piece ginger, peeled, minced
- 2 tablespoons of ghee
- Sea salt and pepper to taste

Directions:

Rub the oxtails with seasonings. Set your instant pot to sauté mode and add in the ghee. Add in the oxtails into instant pot and brown them on all sides. Toss in the garlic, onion, jalapeno, carrot, ginger and continue to sauté for a few minutes. Set the instant pot to keep warm/cancel setting to stop sauté mode. Add remaining ingredients into instant pot and set to meat/stew setting for 40 minutes. Once done release pressure naturally. Stir the ingredients. Divide into serving dishes. Serve.

Nutritional Information per serving:

Calories: 303   Fat: 24g   Fiber: 2g   Carbs: 3g   Protein: 33g

Chapter 4. Pork Instant Pot Recipes

41. Apple Cider Pork

Cook Time: 25 minutes   **Servings: 4**

Ingredients:

- 2lbs. pork loin
- 2 tablespoons extra virgin olive oil
- 2 cups apple cider
- 1 yellow onion, peeled, chopped
- 1 tablespoon onion flakes, dried
- 2 apples, cored and chopped
- Salt and pepper to taste

Directions:

Set your instant pot on the sauté mode, add the oil, and heat it up. Add the pork, dried onion, salt, pepper, and stir. Brown the meat on all sides and transfer to a plate. Add the onion to the instant pot, stir and cook for 2 minutes. Add cider, apples, salt and pepper, and return the meat to the instant pot. Stir. Cover and cook on Manual mode for 20 minutes. Release the pressure naturally, and uncover the instant pot. Transfer pork to cutting board, slice and divide amongst serving dishes. Add the sauce and mix from instant pot. Serve.

Nutritional Information per serving:

Calories: 450   Fat: 22g   Fiber: 2.2g   Carbs: 9g   Protein: 37.2g

42. Pork Sausages & Sweet Potatoes

Cook Time: 15 minutes   **Servings: 6**

Ingredients:

For the sweet potatoes:

- 4 sweet potatoes, peeled and cut into cubes
- 1 teaspoon dry mustard
- Salt and pepper to taste
- 1 tablespoon butter
- 4-ounces milk, warmed
- 6-ounces water

For the sausages:

- 6 pork sausages
- 1 tablespoon of cornstarch mixed with one tablespoon water
- Salt and pepper to taste
- 3-ounces water
- 3-ounces red wine
- ½ cup onion jam
- 2 tablespoons extra virgin olive oil

Directions:

Place the sweet potatoes into the instant pot, add 6-ounces water, salt, pepper, stir and cover, and cook on steam mode for 5 minutes. Release the pressure with quick-release. Drain the sweet potatoes and place them in a bowl. Add the milk and butter, mustard, more salt and pepper and mash them well. Set the dish aside.

Set your instant pot to sauté mode, add the oil and heat it up. Add the sausages and brown them on all sides. Add the onion jam, wine, 3-ounces of water, salt and pepper. Cover the instant pot and cook on the meat/stew setting for 8 minutes. Release the pressure with quick-release and divide the sausages among serving plates. Add cornstarch to mixture in instant pot and stir well. Drizzle the sauce from instant pot over the sausages and serve with mashed sweet potatoes.

43. Sausage & Red Beans
Cooking Time: 30 minutes
Servings: 8
Ingredients:

- 1 lb. smoked sausage, sliced
- 1 bay leaf
- 1 lb. red beans, dried, soaked overnight and drained
- 2 tablespoons Cajun seasoning
- 1 celery stalk, chopped
- Salt and pepper to taste
- ½ green bell pepper, seeded, chopped
- 1 small yellow onion, peeled, chopped
- 1 garlic clove, peeled, chopped
- ¼ teaspoon cumin
- 5 cups water
- 1 teaspoon parsley, dried

Directions:
In your instant pot mix the beans, bay leaf, sausage, Cajun seasoning, celery, salt, bell pepper, parsley, cumin, garlic, onion, pepper, water and stir. Cover and cook on Bean/Chili setting for 30 minutes. Release the pressure using quick-release, uncover the instant pot, divide and mix into serving bowls. Serve.
Nutritional Information per serving:
Calories: 248   Fat: 15g   Fiber: 12.3g   Carbs: 4g   Protein: 29g

44. Kalua Pork
Cooking Time: 90 minutes
Servings: 5
Ingredients:

- 4 lbs. pork shoulder, cut into half
- ½ cup water
- 1 tablespoon liquid smoke
- 2 tablespoons coconut oil
- Salt and pepper to taste
- Steamed green beans, for serving

Directions:
Set your instant pot on the sauté mode, add the oil and heat it up. Add in the pork, salt and pepper. Brown the meat for 3 minutes on each side. Transfer meat to a plate. Add the water and liquid smoke to the instant pot and stir. Return the meat to the instant pot and stir ingredients and cover with lid. Cook on Meat/Stew setting for 90 minutes. Release the pressure on quick-release, and transfer meat to cutting board and shred with 2 forks. Divide the pork onto serving plates, add some sauce on top, and serve with steamed green beans on the side.
Nutritional Information per serving:
Calories: 243   Fat: 18g   Fiber: 1g   Carbs: 5g   Protein: 29g

45. Pork with Hominy

Cooking Time: 30 minutes **Servings: 6**

Ingredients:

- 1 ¼ lbs. pork shoulder, boneless, cut into medium pieces
- 2 tablespoons chili powder
- 2 tablespoons almond oil
- Salt and pepper to taste
- 1 white onion, peeled, chopped
- 4 garlic cloves, peeled, minced
- 30 ounces canned hominy, drained
- 4 cups beef stock
- Avocado slices, for serving
- Lime wedges, for serving
- 2 tablespoons cornstarch
- ¼ cup water

Directions:

Set your instant pot on the sauté mode, add one tablespoon of almond oil and heat it. Add the pork, salt, pepper, and brown the meat on all sides. Transfer the meat to a bowl. Add the rest of the almond oil to the instant pot and heat it up. Add the garlic, chili powder, onion, stir and sauté for 4 minutes. Add half of the beef stock, stir and cook for 1 minute. Add the rest of the stock and return the pork to the instant pot. Stir and cover, and cook on Manual setting for 30 minutes.

Release the pressure naturally for 10 minutes. Transfer the pork to a cutting board, shred it using 2 forks. Add the cornstarch into instant pot, mixed with water. Set instant pot on sauté mode. Add the hominy, more salt, and pepper, and the shredded pork, stir and cook for 2 minutes. Divide among serving bowls. Serve with avocado slices and lime wedges.

Nutritional Information per serving:

Calories: 250   Fat: 8.7g   Fiber: 7.7g   Carbs: 2g   Protein: 32g

46. Pork Tostadas

Cook Time: 30 minutes **Servings: 4**

Ingredients:

- 4 lbs. pork shoulder, boneless, cubed
- 2 cups diet cola
- ½ cup picante sauce
- 2 teaspoons chili powder
- 2 tablespoons tomato paste
- ¼ teaspoon cumin
- 1 cup enchilada sauce
- Corn tortillas, for serving
- Mexican cheese, shredded, for serving
- Shredded lettuce, for serving
- Guacamole, for serving

Directions:

In your instant pot mix 1 cup of diet cola with picante sauce, salsa, tomato paste, chili powder, cumin and stir. Add the pork, stir and cover. Cook on Meat/Stew setting for 25 minutes. Release pressure naturally. Uncover the instant pot, drain juice from instant pot, transfer the meat to a cutting board. Shred the meat with 2 forks. Return the meat to instant pot. Add in remaining diet cola and enchilada sauce, stir. Set the instant pot to sauté mode and heat well. Serve with tortillas, lettuce, cheese and guacamole.

Nutritional Information per serving:

Calories: 160   Fat: 13g   Fiber: 3g   Carbs: 6g   Protein: 9g

47. Pork Tamales
Cook Time: 1 hour and 35 minutes   **Servings: 24 pieces**
Ingredients:

- 8-ounces dried corn husks, soaked for 1 day and drained
- 4 cups water
- 3lbs. pork shoulder, boneless, cubed
- 1 yellow onion, peeled, chopped
- 3 tablespoons chili powder
- 2 garlic cloves, peeled, crushed
- 1 teaspoon baking soda
- ¼ cup shortening
- ¼ cup almond oil
- 4 cups masa
- 1 teaspoon cumin
- Salt and pepper to taste

Directions:

In your instant pot, mix 2 cups of water with onion, garlic, chili powder, salt, pepper, and cumin. Add in the pork and stir, cover the instant pot. Cook on the Meat/Stew setting for 75 minutes. Release the pressure naturally. Transfer the meat to a cutting board and shred it with 2 forks. Place pork in a bowl. Add one tablespoon of the cooking liquid from instant pot. Add more salt and pepper and set aside. In a bowl mix salt, pepper, masa, baking powder, shortening and almond oil. Combine using hand mixer. Add the cooking liquid from the instant pot and blend well. Add 2 cups water to instant pot.

Place the steamer basket inside of instant pot. Unfold 2 of the corn husks, place them on a work surface, add ¼ cup of the masa mixture near top of husk, press into a square and leave 2-inches at the bottom. Add 1 tablespoon pork in the center of the masa, wrap the husk around the dough and place it standing up in the steamer basket. Repeat with the rest of the husks, cover the instant pot and cook on the Steam setting for 20 minutes. Release the pressure naturally. Remove the tamales and place them on serving plates. Serve.

Nutritional Information per serving:
Calories: 150   Fat: 17.2g   Fiber: 2g   Carbs: 11g   Protein: 7g

48. Pork Carnitas
Cook Time: 1 hour and 10 minutes   **Servings: 8**
Ingredients:

- 3 lbs. pork shoulder, chopped
- 2 tablespoons ghee
- 1 jalapeno pepper, chopped
- 1 poblano pepper, seeded, chopped
- 1 green bell pepper
- 3 garlic cloves, minced
- 1 lb. tomatillos, cut into quarters
- 1 yellow onion, chopped
- 2 bay leaves
- 2 cups beef stock
- 1 red onion, chopped, for serving
- Cheddar cheese, shredded, for serving
- 1 teaspoon oregano, dried
- Salt and pepper to taste
- 1 teaspoon cumin
- Flour tortillas, for serving

Directions:

Set your instant pot on the sauté mode, add the ghee and heat it up. Add in the pork, salt and pepper. Brown the meat on all sides for about 3 minutes. Add the bell pepper, jalapeno pepper, poblano pepper, tomatillos, onion, oregano, garlic, cumin, bay leaves and stock. Stir and cover, cooking on the Meat/Stew setting for 55 minutes. Release the pressure naturally for 10 minutes. Transfer the meat to cutting board. Puree the mix from instant pot with immersion blender. Shred meat with 2 forks.

Add the meat back into the instant pot with the puree mix. Divide the pork mixture onto flour tortillas on serving plates. Add onion, cheese and serve.

Nutritional Information per serving:
Calories: 355   Fat: 23g   Fiber: 1g   Carbs: 10g   Protein: 23g

---

49. Instant Pot Balsamic Pork Tenderloin

Cook Time: 25 minutes   **Servings: 4**

Ingredients:

- 2 lbs. pork tenderloin
- 2 tablespoons coconut oil
- 1 cup chicken stock
- ¼ cup balsamic vinegar
- 2 cloves of garlic, minced

- 1 tablespoon Worcestershire sauce
- ¼ cup water
- Sea salt and black pepper to taste
- 1 teaspoon sage, ground
- 1 tablespoon Dijon mustard

Directions:

Set your instant pot to the sauté mode, add the coconut oil and heat. Add the pork and brown the meat on all sides for five minutes. Add the remaining ingredients, and set to Manual setting for 20 minutes. When cooking is complete, release the pressure naturally in 10-minutes. Cut the pork into medallions and place on serving plates, cover with sauce from instant pot. Serve hot!

Nutritional Information per serving:
Calories: 347   Fat: 26g   Fiber: 1g   Carbs: 3g   Protein: 33g

---

50. Asian Pork Short Ribs

Cooking Time: 60 minutes   **Servings: 4**

Ingredients:

- 4 lbs. pork short ribs
- 2 green onions, chopped
- 1 teaspoon coconut oil
- 3 garlic cloves, minced
- 3 ginger slices

- ½ cup water
- 2 teaspoons sesame oil
- 1/4 cup rice wine
- ½ cup soy sauce

Directions:

Set your instant pot onto saute mode, add coconut oil and heat it up. Add the green onions, ginger, garlic, and stir and cook for 1 minute. Add the ribs, water, wine, sesame oil and soy sauce. Stir and cook for 3 minutes. Cover the instant pot and cook on the Meat/Stew setting for 45 minutes. Release the pressure naturally for 15 minutes. Uncover the instant pot and transfer the ribs to a plate. Strain the liquid from the instant pot, divide the ribs among serving plates and drizzle with sauce.

51. Ribs & Coleslaw

Cooking Time: 35 minutes   **Servings: 4**

Ingredients:
- 2 ½ lbs. pork baby back ribs
- 1 teaspoon onion powder
- ½ teaspoon garlic powder
- ½ teaspoon chili powder

- ½ teaspoon dry mustard
- ½ teaspoon paprika
- Salt and pepper to taste
- 2 tablespoons almond oil

For the sauce:
- ½ teaspoon smoked paprika
- 1/3 cup apple cider vinegar
- ¼ cup coconut Aminos
- 2 garlic cloves, minced
- ¾ cup tomato paste

- 6-ounces tomato paste
- 2 bacon slices, chopped
- 1 small yellow onion, chopped
- ½ cup water
- Salt and pepper to taste

For the coleslaw:
- 2 green onions, chopped
- 2 carrots, grated
- Salt and pepper to taste
- 2 ½ teaspoons caraway seeds

- 3 cups green cabbage, shredded
- 1 cup red cabbage, shredded
- ¾ cup mayonnaise
- ¼ cup apple cider vinegar

Directions:
In a salad bowl, mix the green onions, carrots, with the cabbage. In a small bowl mix the caraway seeds with the mayonnaise, salt, pepper, ¼ cup vinegar and stir well. Pour over the coleslaw, and toss to coat, keep in fridge until ready to serve. In a bowl mix onion powder, paprika, dry mustard, garlic powder, chili powder, salt and pepper. Rub the ribs with this mixture. Set your instant pot to sauté mode, add in almond oil and heat it. Add the bacon and cook until done. Add in onion and garlic and cook for an additional five minutes. Place the ribs into your instant pot. Add some water, cover and cook on the Meat/Stew setting for 15 minutes. Add the remaining ingredients for ribs into instant pot and cook for another 10 minutes. Release the pressure naturally for 15 minutes. Transfer the ribs to a plate. Remove some of the sauce, leave enough in pot to cover bottom. Then place layer of ribs into instant pot and cover with layer of sauce until all the ribs are in the instant pot. Cover and cook on Manual setting for 10 minutes. Release pressure again, and divide the ribs among serving plates, and serve with coleslaw.

Nutritional Information per serving:
Calories: 360 Fat: 15g Fiber: 1g Carbs: 4g Protein: 17g

52. Country-style Ribs
Cooking Time: 20 minutes
Servings: 8
Ingredients:

- 5 lbs. country-style ribs, boneless

For the brine:

- 1 tablespoon Truvia sweetener
- Salt to taste
- 4 cups water
- 3 garlic cloves, crushed
- 2 tablespoons liquid smoke

For the ribs:

- 2 tablespoons butter
- ½ tablespoon water
- 1 cup onion, chopped
- Cayenne pepper
- 1 teaspoon chili powder
- ½ teaspoon cinnamon, ground
- 2 apples, peeled, cored, sliced

For the sauce:

- 2 tablespoons yellow mustard
- 1 tablespoon liquid smoke
- 1 tablespoon Worcestershire sauce
- 1 teaspoon hot sauce
- 1 tablespoon Truvia
- 2 tablespoons Dijon mustard
- 2 tablespoons cornstarch
- 1 tablespoon soy sauce
- ¼ cup honey
- 2 tablespoons water

Directions:

In a bowl, mix the 4 cups water with some salt, and 1 tablespoon Truvia, garlic, and 2 tablespoons liquid smoke. Stir, and add the pork ribs and keep them in fridge to marinate for 2 hours. Set your instant pot to the saute mode, add 2 tablespoons butter and melt it. Add the ribs and brown them on all sides. Transfer the ribs to a plate. Add the onions, ½ tablespoon water, stir, and cook for 2 minutes. Add the cinnamon, cayenne, chili powder, and apple slices. Return the ribs to the instant pot, cover and cook on the Meat/Stew setting for 15 minutes. Release pressure naturally. Transfer the ribs to a plate. Puree the onions and apples using a food processor, and set the instant pot on saute mode again. Add the yellow mustard, 1 tablespoon liquid smoke, Dijon mustard, 1 tablespoon Truvia, Worcestershire sauce, hot sauce, soy sauce, honey and stir well. Add cornstarch mixed with 2 tablespoons of water, and cook for 2 minutes. Divide the ribs onto serving plates and drizzle with sauce. Serve.

Nutritional Information per serving:
Calories: 470   Fat: 34g   Fiber: 3g   Carbs: 10g   Protein: 29g

53. Pork Chops & Spinach Salad
Cook Time: 20 minutes   **Servings: 6**
Ingredients:
For the pork chops:
- 6 pork chops, boneless
- 2 cups beef stock
- 3 garlic cloves, chopped
- 1 yellow onion, chopped

- 1 bunch mixed sage, rosemary, oregano, thyme
- 2 tablespoons ghee
- 1 teaspoon smoked paprika
- Salt and pepper to taste

For Spinach Salad:
- 1 large package of spinach leaves
- 1 English cucumber, sliced
- ½ red onion, thinly sliced

- Balsamic Vinegar dressing
- 2 large tomatoes, diced

Directions:
Set your instant pot to the sauté mode, and add in the ghee and heat it up. Add in the pork chops and brown them on all sides. Add the rest of the ingredients for porkchops into the instant pot. Set the instant pot to the Meat/Stew setting for 15 minutes. Meanwhile prepare the spinach salad in a large salad bowl adding all ingredients except for the dressing then keep in the fridge until ready to serve, just before serving add dressing and toss to mix. Release the pressure naturally. Put the pork chops onto a plate and remove and discard the herbs from instant pot. Place the pork chops back into pot and place on Manual mode, for 2 minutes. Stir. Divide the pork chops on serving plates along with spinach salad.
Nutritional Information per serving:
Calories: 410   Fat: 20g   Carbs: 9g   Protein: 30.2g

---

54. Pork Chops & Brown Rice
Cooking Time: 25 minutes   **Servings: 6**
Ingredients:
- 2 lbs. pork chops
- 2 hot peppers, minced
- 1 tablespoon peppercorns, crushed
- 2 cups brown rice
- 3 garlic cloves, crushed

- 1 cup onion, chopped
- 2 ½ cups beef stock
- Salt and ground pepper to taste
- 3 tablespoons butter

Directions:
Set your instant pot to the sauté mode, add the butter and melt it. Add in garlic and onions, hot peppers and pork chops. Brown the meat on all sides. Remove the pork chops from instant pot once they are browned and place on a plate. Add the rice and beef stock to instant pot and stir. Add the porkchops back to the pot and set instant pot to the Meat/Stew setting for 25 minutes. Release the pressure naturally for 10 minutes. Add salt and pepper and divide porkchops and rice among serving plates. Serve.
Nutritional Information per serving:
Calories: 430   Fat: 12.3g   Fiber: 4.3g   Carbs: 3g   Protein: 30g

55. Braised Pork

Cooking Time: 75 minutes   **Servings: 6**

Ingredients:

- 4 lbs. pork butt, chopped
- 16-ounces red wine
- 16-ounces beef stock
- 4-ounces lemon juice
- 2 tablespoons extra virgin olive oil
- 1 tablespoon paprika
- ¼ cup garlic powder
- ¼ cup onion, chopped
- Salt and pepper to taste

Directions:

In your instant pot mix the pork with the stock, wine, lemon juice, garlic powder, onion, oil, paprika, salt and pepper. Stir and cover, setting to the Meat/Stew mode for 45 minutes. Release the pressure naturally for 15 minutes. Stir the pork, divide into serving bowls. Serve.

Nutritional Information per serving:

Calories: 452   Fat: 44g   Fiber: 1g   Carbs: 12g   Protein: 27g

56. Chinese Barbecue Pork

Cooking Time: 50 minutes   **Servings: 6**

Ingredients:

- 2lbs. pork belly
- 2 tablespoons dry sherry
- 4 tablespoons soy sauce
- 1-quart beef stock
- 2 teaspoons sesame oil
- 2 teaspoons Truvia
- 1 teaspoon peanut oil

Directions:

Set your instant pot on the Manual mode, add the sherry, stock, soy sauce and stir and cook for 8 minutes. Add the pork, stir, cover and cook on the Meat/Stew setting for 30 minutes. Release the pressure naturally, transfer the pork to a cutting board, allow to cool and chop into smaller pieces. Add the sauce in instant pot into a bowl and set aside. Set your instant pot to sauté mode, add in the peanut oil and add the pork back into the instant pot. Cook for a few minutes browning all sides of the meat. In a bowl mix the sesame oil with the sauce that was put aside and mix well. Add this mix to the instant pot and stir. Set on Manual mode for 10 minutes. Divide the pork onto serving plates, drizzle with sauce. Serve.

Nutritional Information per serving:

Calories: 398   Fat: 22g   Fiber: 1g   Carbs: 5g   Protein: 43g

57. Pork Roast with Fennel

Cooking Time: 1 hour and 20 minutes   **Servings: 4**

Ingredients:

- 2 lbs. pork meat, boneless
- 5-ounces white wine
- 1 yellow onion, chopped
- 2 garlic cloves, minced

- Salt and pepper to taste
- 2 tablespoons extra virgin olive oil
- 5-ounces beef stock
- 1 lb. fennel bulbs, sliced

Directions:

Set your instant pot to the sauté mode, add the oil and heat it up. Add the pork, salt and pepper, stir and brown meat on all sides. Add the wine, garlic and stock to the instant pot. Cook for another few minutes. Transfer the pork to a plate. Stir the sauce in instant pot well. Return pork to pot, cover and cook on Manual setting for 40 minutes. Release the pressure naturally in 15 minutes. Add the onion, and fennel, to instant pot stir and cover. Cook on the Manual setting for 15 minutes. Release pressure again, stir and transfer the pork to serving plates. Serve with onion and fennel on the side with the cooking sauce from the instant pot drizzled over.

Nutritional Information per serving:

Calories: 426   Fat: 15g   Fiber: 1.2g   Carbs: 7g   Protein: 36g

58. Pulled Pork

Cook Time: 1 hour and 20 minutes
Servings: 6
Ingredients:

- 3 lbs. pork shoulder, boneless, cut into chunks
- 8-ounces of water
- 1 tablespoon Truvia
- 2 teaspoons dry mustard
- 2 teaspoons smoked paprika

For the sauce:

- 4-ounces hot water
- 2 teaspoons dry mustard
- Cayenne Pepper
- Salt and pepper to taste
- 2 teaspoons Truvia
- 12-ounces apple cider vinegar

Directions:

Mix the Truvia with smoked paprika, 2 teaspoons dry mustard, and salt in a bowl. Rub the pork with this mixture and place the pork pieces into your instant pot. Add the 8-ounces of water and stir. Cover the instant pot and cook on the Meat/Stew setting for 75 minutes. Release the pressure naturally within 10 minutes. Transfer the pork to a cutting board and shred it using 2 forks. Discard half the cooking liquid from instant pot. In a bowl mix the 2 teaspoons of Truvia for sauce, with vinegar, cayenne, salt, pepper and hot water along with 2 teaspoons of dry mustard and stir well. Add to instant pot along with cooking sauce and cook on Manual for 3 minutes. Release the pressure naturally, and divide the pork among serving plates and drizzle with sauce from instant pot. Serve.

Nutritional Information per serving:

Calories: 428   Fat: 11g   Fiber: 4g   Carbs: 3g   Protein: 31g

59. Creamy Pork Chops
Cooking Time: 20 minutes
Servings: 4
Ingredients:

- 4 pork chops, boneless
- 2 tablespoons extra virgin olive oil
- ½ small bunch of fresh parsley, chopped
- Salt and pepper to taste
- 1 cup sour cream
- 10-ounce can of cream of mushroom soup
- 2 teaspoons of chicken bouillon
- 1 cup water

Directions:
Set your instant pot to the sauté mode, add the oil and heat it up. Add in the pork chops, pepper and salt. Brown the meat on all sides. Transfer pork chops to a plate. Add the water and bouillon to the instant pot and stir well. Return the pork chops to the instant pot, cover and cook on Manual setting for 9 minutes. Release the pressure naturally, transfer the pork chops to a platter and set aside. Set the instant pot on Manual mode and heat up the cooking liquid. Add the mushroom soup, stir and cook for 2 minutes. Add the parsley and sour cream, stir and mix well. Pour over pork chops. Serve.

Nutritional Information per serving:
Calories: 282 Fat: 14g Fiber: 1g Carbs: 9g Protein: 22g

60. Pork Chops and Onion
Cooking Time: 15 minutes
Servings: 4
Ingredients:

- 4 pork chops
- 1 lb. onions, sliced
- ½ cup milk
- 2 tablespoons extra virgin olive oil
- 1 garlic clove, minced
- 2 tablespoons parsley, fresh, chopped
- Salt and pepper to taste
- ½ cup white wine
- 1 tablespoon flour
- 2 tablespoons cornstarch mixed with 3 tablespoons water
- 2 tablespoons butter
- 2 tablespoons lime juice

Directions:
Set your instant pot on the sauté mode, add the oil and butter and heat up. Add the pork chops, salt and pepper. Brown the meat on all sides. Transfer meat to a plate. Add the onion, garlic to the instant pot and stir, cook for 2 minutes. Add the lime juice, wine, milk, parsley, and return the pork chops to the instant pot. Stir, cover and cook on Manual setting for 15 minutes. Release the pressure, add the cornstarch and flour, stir well. Cook on Manual mode for 3 minutes. Divide pork chops on serving plates drizzle with sauce. Serve.

Nutritional Information per serving:
Calories: 212 Fat: 16g Fiber: 3g Carbs: 8g Protein: 19g

61. Apple Cider Pork
Cooking Time: 25 minutes
Servings: 4
Ingredients:

- 2 lbs. pork loin
- 2 tablespoons coconut oil
- 2 cups apple cider
- 1 yellow onion, chopped
- 2 apples, cored, chopped
- 1 tablespoon onion flakes, dried
- Salt and pepper to taste

Directions:
Set your instant pot to the sauté mode, add the coconut oil and heat it up. Add the pork loin, salt and pepper, along with the dried onion. Brown the meat on all sides. Transfer to a plate. Add the onion to instant pot and stir for 2 minutes. Add the cider and return the meat to the instant pot, adding chopped apples, more salt and pepper. Cover and cook on Manual mode for 20 minutes. Release the pressure, naturally, and transfer the pork to cutting board, slice it. Divide the pork among serving plates. Add the sauce from instant pot and serve.

Nutritional Information per serving:
Calories: 432   Fat: 21g   Fiber: 2.2g   Carbs: 6g   Protein: 36g

---

62. Bacon and Egg Omelette
Cook Time: 8 minutes
Servings: 4
Ingredients:

- 5 slices of bacon, chopped into small pieces
- 5 free range eggs
- 1 tablespoon parsley, fresh, chopped
- 2 tablespoons of coconut oil
- Salt and pepper to taste

Directions:
Lightly beat your eggs in a mixing bowl with a fork. Add a dash of salt and pepper. Set your instant pot to the sauté mode, add the coconut oil and heat it up. Add the pieces of bacon and sauté them until they are cooked and slightly crispy for about 5 minutes. Add the mixed eggs and stir into the bacon. Leave the eggs for about 3 minutes or until they are done to your liking. Remove eggs from pot and add to serving plates, and sprinkle tops with chopped parsley. Serve.

Nutritional Information per serving:
Calories: 227   Fat: 14g   Fiber: 1g   Carbs: 2g   Protein: 20g

63. Ham Hock Soup

Cook Time: *1 hour and 10 minutes*

Servings: *8*

Ingredients:
- 1 ham hock
- 2 celery stalks, chopped
- 1 onion, chopped
- 2 carrots, chopped
- 2 litres of water

Directions:

Place your ham hock into your instant pot, and sprinkle with salt and pepper, can cover with water. Press the Meat/Stew button and set for 40 minutes. Once it is done, release the pressure naturally, then remove the lid. Remove the ham hock to a cutting board. Remove the meat from the ham hock and replace it back into the instant pot. Add the onion, carrot, and celery to the pot and secure the lid. Press the "Soup" button and set for 30 minutes. Release the pressure once again when it is done, naturally. Stir the soup and serve hot!

Nutritional Information per serving:

Calories: 223   Fat: 11g   Fiber: 2g   Carbs: 1g   Protein: 30g

---

64. Bacon, Spinach & Mozzarella Bundles

Cook Time: *6 minutes*

Servings: *12 bundles (3 per person)*

Ingredients:
- 12 slices of bacon
- 250 g mozzarella cheese, cut into 12 even pieces
- 2 tablespoons extra-virgin olive oil
- Large handful of baby spinach leaves

Directions:

Wrap each piece of mozzarella cheese in spinach leaves, about 4 pieces per piece. Wrap each spinach-coated piece with a piece of bacon. Your bundles should look like round bacon-covered balls. Select the sauté mode on your instant pot. Add the oil to the pot and heat. Add the bundles in groups of 6. Cook on either side for 3 minutes each or until golden and sizzling. Serve hot!

Nutritional Information per serving:

Calories: 232   Fat: 19g   Fiber: 2g   Carbs: 3g   Protein: 33g

---

65. Keto Carbonara with Bacon & Cream

Cooking Time: *10 minutes*

Serving: *4*

Ingredients:
- 5 zucchinis, spiralized as a fettucine-style pasta alternative
- 4 strips of bacon, chopped into small pieces
- ¼ cup grated parmesan cheese
- 1 cup heavy cream
- 1 garlic clove, finely chopped
- 2 tablespoons extra virgin olive oil

Directions:

Select your sauté mode on your instant pot, add the oil and heat it up. Add in the bacon pieces and garlic into instant pot. Cook until they are sizzling for about 3 minutes. Add the zucchini pasta and coat with oil and bacon. Saute zucchini for about 2 minutes. Add cream and parmesan cheese and cream and stir. Cook for another 5 minutes and continue to stir. Turn off your instant pot. Serve Carbonara hot!

Nutritional Information per serving:
Calories: 263   Fat: 20g   Fiber: 1g   Carbs: 3g   Protein: 31g

66. Chorizo Sausage with Feta, Spicy Tomatoes & Spinach

Cook Time: 12 minutes   **Servings: 4**

Ingredients:
- 5 chorizo sausages, cut into small chunks
- 4 large tomatoes
- 2 handfuls of baby spinach
- 150gm feta cheese, cut into small cubes
- 1 teaspoon chilli flakes
- 2 tablespoons coconut oil
- Olive oil to drizzle on top of tomatoes

Directions:
Turn the oven on to broil, hi temperature. Cut tomatoes in half and drizzle tops with olive oil, salt, pepper and chilli. Place the tomatoes on baking tray on upper rack in oven. Select sauté mode on your instant pot, add the coconut oil and heat. Add the Chorizo sausage to instant pot and stir. Cook sausage for 5 minutes, when it begins to brown add in the spinach and feta and stir. When tomatoes are browned and soft remove from oven. Turn off the instant pot and serve Chorizo mixture. Serve with tomato halves.

Nutritional Information per serving:
Calories: 273   Fat: 20g   Fiber: 1g   Carbs: 3g   Protein: 32g

67. Sautéed Asparagus with Bacon

Cook Time: 15 minutes   **Servings: 4**

Ingredients:
- 4 strips of bacon
- 16 spears of asparagus (4 per person)
- 2 tablespoons of butter
- 1 garlic clove, minced

Directions:
Select the sauté mode on your instant pot. Add the butter and heat it. Add the minced garlic and the bacon strips and sauté until crispy for about 5 minutes. Add in the asparagus spears and stir and coat them, and cook for an additional 10 minutes. Place on serving plates with some salt and pepper to taste. Serve.

Nutritional Information per serving:
Calories: 223   Fat: 12g   Fiber: 3g   Carbs: 7g   Protein: 26g

68. Instant Pot Scrambled Egg & Sausage

Cook Time: 17 minutes   **Servings: 4**

Ingredients:
- 1 lb. ground sausage
- 8 large eggs

- 2 tablespoons extra virgin olive oil
- 1 green bell pepper, seeded, diced
- 1 red bell pepper, seeded, diced
- 1 yellow bell pepper, seeded, diced
- 1 large onion, diced
- ¼ cup heavy cream
- Salt and pepper to taste

Directions:

Set your instant pot to the sauté mode, add the oil, and add the onions and bell peppers and cook for five minutes. Add the sausage, stir and select the Manual function at low pressure and choose 10-minute cook time. Once the cook time is done, do a quick-release of pressure. Discard any excess fat in instant pot. Whisk your eggs, heavy cream, salt and pepper. Pour the egg mixture over the sausage mixture. Close the instant pot and select Manual function at low pressure and choose a 2-minute cook time. Divide into serving dishes. Serve.

Nutritional Information per serving:

Calories: 231   Fat: 14g   Fiber: 2g   Carbs: 2g   Protein: 28g

---

69. *Instant Pot Split Pea & Ham Soup*

Cook Time: *17 minutes*   **Servings:** *4*

Ingredients:

- ½ cup ham, diced
- 2 cups dried peas
- 5 cups of water
- 1 teaspoon onion, finely chopped
- Salt and pepper to taste
- 1 cup carrots, peeled, sliced

Directions:

Place all your ingredients into your instant pot. Select the Manual mode and set for a cook time of 17 minutes. Divide soup up into serving bowls. Serve hot!

Nutritional Information per serving:

Calories: 216   Fat: 14g   Fiber: 2.2g   Carbs: 7g   Protein: 24g

---

70. *Instant Pot Pork Feet & Soy Bean Soup*

Cook Time: *1 hour*   **Servings:** *4*

Ingredients:

- 2 lbs. pork feet
- 1 cup soaked soy beans
- 6 cups water
- 3 thin slices of ginger
- Salt and pepper to taste
- 2 green onion leaves, minced

Directions:

Add all your ingredients into your instant pot, except the minced green onion leaves. Select the soup mode and cook time for an hour. When soup is done divide it up into serving bowls and top with minced green leaves. Serve hot!

Nutritional Information per serving:

Calories: 228   Fat: 23g   Fiber: 1g   Carbs: 7g   Protein: 35g

Chapter 5. Lamb-Based Instant Pot Recipes

71. *Instant Pot Lamb Curry*
Cook Time: 20 minutes　　　　　　　**Servings: 6**
Ingredients:

- 1 ½ lbs. lamb stew meat, cubed
- 4 cloves of garlic, minced
- Cilantro, chopped
- 1 medium zucchini, diced
- 3 medium carrots, sliced
- 1 medium onion, diced
- ¾ teaspoon turmeric

- 1 ½ tablespoon garam masala
- 1 (14-ounce can) tomatoes, diced
- 1 tablespoon ghee
- Sea salt and pepper to taste
- Juice of ½ a lime
- ½ cup coconut milk
- 1-inch piece ginger, fresh, grated

Directions:
Combine your meat, grated ginger, minced garlic, lime juice, coconut milk, sea salt and pepper in a container with a lid. Mix ingredients and marinated in the fridge for 30 minutes.

After marinating is complete, add the meat, tomatoes with their juice, marinade, ghee, garam masala, carrots and onions to your instant pot. Lock the lid in place, then set the steam release handle to 'Sealing' then select the Manual mode and cook at high pressure for 20 minutes. Once the cooking time is complete, allow your instant pot to release pressure naturally for 15 minutes, then flip the steam release handle to 'Venting' to release remaining steam before you attempt to open the lid. Remove the lid then set your instant pot to the sauté mode in the normal setting. Stir in the diced zucchini and simmer for 5-6 minutes without the lid or until the zucchini is tender and the sauce has thickened. Divide into serving dishes, over cauliflower rice, and garnish with chopped cilantro. Serve hot!

Nutritional Information per serving:
Calories: 230　Fat: 9g　Fiber: 3g　Carbs: 1g　Protein: 25g

72. *Instant Pot Lamb Curry with Yogurt*
Cooking Time: 25 minutes　　　　　**Servings: 4**
Ingredients:

- 2 lbs. lamb, boneless, cubed
- 4 Chile pepper, chopped
- 2 tablespoons clarified butter
- 1 onion, diced

- 4 cups plain yogurt
- 1 teaspoon cumin seed
- 2 teaspoons ground turmeric
- 2 tablespoons coriander seeds

Directions:
Add the ginger, garlic, chiles, spices and yogurt into a food processor and process until well blended. Spoon the mixture over lamb, tossing to coat, place in fridge for 3 hours to marinate. Set your instant pot on sauté mode, add butter and heat it up. Add in the onions and brown them. Once onion is browned add in the lamb and yogurt marinade and mix. Place lid on instant pot and set to Meat/Stew setting for 20 minutes. Release pressure naturally for 15 minutes. Divide between serving dishes. Serve.

Calories: 260   Fat: 23g   Fiber: 12g   Carbs: 7g   Protein: 22g

---

73. *Instant Pot Mediterranean Lamb Roast*

Cooking Time: 60 minutes   **Servings: 6**

Ingredients:

- 4 lbs. lamb shanks
- 2 tablespoons olive oil
- 2 cups beef broth
- 1 teaspoon thyme
- 3 large sweet potatoes, peeled, cubed
- 1 teaspoon ginger
- 3 cloves garlic, minced
- 1 teaspoon sage
- 1 teaspoon marjoram
- Sea salt and pepper to taste

Directions:

Set your instant pot to sauté mode, add the oil and heat it. Add the lamb and swirl it around to coat with oil. Sear one side of lamb then flip it over to sear the other side. Sprinkle lamb shanks with all the herbs, sea salt, pepper and add broth. Cover the instant pot and set to Meat/Stew setting for a cook time of 45 minutes. Once cooking is completed release the pressure naturally for 10 minutes. Add the diced sweet potatoes. Close instant pot and set an additional cook time of 10 minutes on Meat/Stew setting. Release pressure again naturally for 10 minutes. Divide into serving dishes. Serve hot!

Nutritional Information per serving:

Calories: 254   Fat: 20g   Fiber: 9g   Carbs: 7g   Protein: 23g

---

74. *Instant Pot Middle Eastern Lamb Stew*

Cooking Time: 1 hour and 9 minutes   **Servings: 4**

Ingredients:

- 1 ½ lbs. lamb stew meat, cubed
- 1 onion, diced
- 2 tablespoons ghee
- 6 garlic cloves, chopped
- ¼ cup raisins
- 1 (15-ounce can) chickpeas, rinsed and drained
- 2 tablespoons honey
- ¼ cup apple cider vinegar
- 2 tablespoons tomato paste
- 1 teaspoon each: coriander, cumin, cinnamon, cumin seeds, sea salt and pepper
- 2 cups chicken stock or broth
- Garnish with fresh cilantro or parsley

Directions:

Set your instant pot to the sauté mode, add the ghee and heat it up. Sauté your onions for about 4 minutes. Add the lamb, spices, garlic, salt and pepper, and sauté for an additional 5 minutes. Brown the meat on all sides. Add the stock, vinegar, tomato paste, honey, chickpeas, and raisins, stir. Cover your instant pot and set to the Meat/Stew setting for 1 hour. Release the pressure naturally for 15 minutes. Remove lid and stir. Serve with cauliflower rice or quinoa and garnish with cilantro or fresh parsley. Divide into serving bowls and serve hot!

Nutritional Information per serving:

Calories: 242   Fat: 18g   Fiber: 2g   Carbs: 6g   Protein: 21g

75. Instant Pot Lamb Rogan Josh

Cooking Time: 15 minutes   **Servings: 4**

Ingredients:

For the lamb:

- 1 ½ lbs. leg of lamb, cubed into small pieces

For the sauce:

- 1 tablespoon coriander, fresh, chopped for garnish
- 2 tablespoons tomato puree
- 1 1/2 cups water
- 2 tomatoes, finely diced
- 1 teaspoon each: ground coriander, ground cumin, ground ginger
- ½ teaspoon chilli, ground

- 4 tablespoons Greek yogurt
- ½ teaspoon garam masala

- ½ teaspoon garam masala
- 2 cloves garlic, minced
- 1 ½ teaspoons fennel seeds
- 1 ½ teaspoons cumin seeds
- 1-inch cinnamon bark
- 3 green cardamom pods, cracked open
- 1 tablespoon olive oil

Directions:

Mix the lamb, garam masala and yogurt for the marinade in a container with lid. Chill in fridge for 24 hours. When ready to begin cooking set your instant pot to the sauté mode, add the oil and all the whole spices. Sizzle and cook until the aromas are released, then in garlic and powdered spices. Cook for about 5 minutes, add in water, tomatoes, and tomato puree, stir. Add in the marinated lamb and stir before cancelling the sauté mode. Place the lid on your instant pot and set on Manual mode for 10 minutes. When cooking is complete press the quick-release to release the pressure. Once the pressure has come down then remove the lid and gently stir the lamb. Add sea salt to taste. Divide into serving dishes and garnish with chopped fresh coriander. Serve over cauliflower rice.

Nutritional Information per serving:

Calories: 231   Fat: 12g   Fiber: 4g   Carbs: 2g   Protein: 23g

76. Instant Pot Leg of Lamb Stew with Dates & Cinnamon

Cook Time: 1 hour and 40 minutes   **Servings: 4**

Ingredients:

- 2 lbs. leg of lamb, boneless
- 1 teaspoon each: black pepper, sea salt, ground cumin powder, ground coriander powder, turmeric powder
- 1 tablespoon balsamic vinegar
- 3 bay leaves
- 1 chicken stock cube
- 1 cup water
- 1 cinnamon stick

- 8 garlic cloves, peeled, whole
- 7 dates, dried
- 4 slices ginger root, fresh
- 1 red onion, sliced
- 1 tablespoon coconut oil
- Cauliflower rice or couscous to serve with
- 1 tablespoon almond flour to thicken sauce

Directions:

Rub the leg of lamb with cumin, coriander seed powder, turmeric, sea salt and pepper. Set your instant pot to the sauté mode, add coconut oil and heat it. Add the lamb and sauté, browning all sides of the meat. Add the onions, ginger around the lamb. Remove the lamb and add remaining ingredients to pot. Stir and bring to a boil. Press the Keep Warm/Cancel setting and return the lamb to the instant pot. Place the lid on the instant pot and set the Manual setting for a cook time of 80 minutes. Once the cook time is complete, release the pressure naturally for 5 minutes, then use the quick-release to let off the rest of the steam.

Remove the lamb to a cutting board, set the instant pot to the sauté mode and allow broth to bubble for 10 minutes, stir it a few times. Cut the lamb meat into bite-size pieces. Add the lamb meat back to the instant pot. Stir the lamb mixture, and turn off the instant pot. If sauce needs to be thickened add in the almond flour. Divide into serving dishes over a bed of cauliflower rice or couscous. Garnish with chopped coriander and serve hot!

Nutritional Information per serving:
Calories: 229   Fat: 11g   Fiber: 3g   Carbs: 3g   Protein: 25g

77. *Lavender Lamb Chops*
Cook Time: 25 minutes   ***Servings: 2***
Ingredients:

- 2 lamb chops, boneless
- 1 tablespoon lavender, chopped
- 2 tablespoons ghee, melted
- 2 tablespoons coconut oil
- 2 tablespoons rosemary, fresh, chopped
- 1 teaspoon garlic, powder
- Zest and juice from 1 lime
- Zest and juice from 1 orange
- 2 cups water
- Sea salt and black pepper to taste

Directions:
Cover the trivet with aluminum foil. Set your instant pot to sauté mode and heat the coconut oil. Sear lamb chops for 2 minutes per side. Remove and set aside. Press the Keep Warm/Cancel button to end sauté mode. In a bowl, add the lavender, ghee, rosemary, orange zest and juice, lime zest and juice and seasonings. Pour 2 cups of water into the instant pot. Place the trivet inside the instant pot. Set the lamb chops on top of it. Close and seal the lid. Select the Manual setting and cook at high-pressure for 15 minutes. When cooking is completed, release the pressure naturally for 15 minutes. Divide onto serving plates. Serve hot!

Nutritional Information per serving:
Calories: 250   Fat: 5g   Dietary Fiber: 1g   Carbohydrates: 5g   Protein: 8g

78. *Leg of Lamb & Spinach Salad*
Cook Time: 40 minutes   ***Servings: 4***
Ingredients:

- 1 tablespoons of ghee
- 3 lbs. leg of lamb, boneless and butterflied
- 2 garlic cloves, minced
- 1 teaspoon cumin, ground
- ¼ teaspoon thyme, dried
- Salt and pepper to taste
- 2 cups vegetable stock

For the salad:
- 4-ounces of feta cheese, crumbled
- ½ cup pecans, toasted
- 1 cup mint, chopped
- 1 ½ tablespoons lemon juice
- 2 cups baby spinach
- ¼ cup olive oil

Directions:

Rub the lamb with salt, pepper, 1 tablespoon melted ghee, thyme, cumin and garlic. Add the stock to your instant pot, add leg of lamb, cover and cook on high for 40 minutes. Leave the leg of lamb on a plate, and slice and divide between serving plates.

In a salad bowl mix the spinach, mint, feta cheese, olive oil, lemon juice, pecans, salt, pepper, and toss then divide amongst serving plates next to the lamb slices. Serve right away.

Nutritional Information per serving:

Calories: 234   Fat: 20g   Fiber: 3g   Carbs: 5g   Protein: 12g

---

79. *Lamb Shanks & Carrots*

Cook Time: 35 minutes   **Servings: 4**

Ingredients:
- 4 lamb shanks
- 2 tablespoons ghee
- 1 yellow onion, chopped
- 3 carrots, sliced
- 1 teaspoon oregano, dried
- 2 tablespoons tomato paste
- 2 garlic cloves, minced
- 2 tablespoons coconut flour
- 4-ounces of beef stock
- 2 tablespoons water
- 1 tomato, chopped
- Sea salt and black pepper to taste

Directions:

In a bowl, mix flour, lamb shanks, salt, pepper, and toss to coat. Set your instant pot to the sauté mode, add the ghee and heat it up. Add the lamb and brown all sides of the meat, then transfer meat to a bowl. Add oregano, carrots, garlic, onion, into instant pot and stir and sauté for 5 minutes. Add the stock, water, tomato paste, tomato and return the lamb to the instant pot. Stir, cover, cook on high for 25 minutes. Divide evenly between serving plates. Serve.

Nutritional Information per serving:

Calories: 400   Fat: 14g   Fiber: 3g   Carbs: 7g   Protein: 30g

---

80. *Lamb & Coconut Curry with Cauliflower Rice*

Cook Time: 28 minutes   **Servings: 6**

Ingredients:
- 3 lbs. lamb, cubed into small pieces
- 2 tablespoons ghee
- 2 cloves garlic, finely chopped
- 1 onion, finely chopped
- 1 teaspoon chilli powder
- ½ teaspoon coriander, ground
- 1 teaspoon cumin, ground
- ½ teaspoon turmeric, ground
- 1 cup full-fat coconut milk
- 1 cup beef stock
- 1 (14-ounce can) tomatoes, chopped

- 1 head of cauliflower, cut into rough chunks
- 1 tablespoon butter

Directions:

On your instant pot select the sauté mode, add the ghee to instant pot and heat. Add the lamb to pot and brown on all sides for about 5 minutes. Add the onion and garlic along with spices to pot and coat the lamb with them by stirring it all together. Add the stock, tomatoes, coconut milk to instant pot.

Change the setting to the Meat/Stew setting and set the cook time for 20 minutes. When the cooking is done, release the pressure naturally for 10 minutes. Meanwhile, add the cauliflower to a food processor and blend until it has the consistency of rice. Tip the cauliflower into a microwave-proof bowl, top with butter, cover and place in the microwave. Cook the cauliflower in the microwave for 3 minutes on high. Stir through the melted butter, adding some sea salt and pepper to taste. Serve the lamb curry on a bed of cauliflower rice.

Nutritional Information per serving:

Calories: 327   Fat: 19g   Fiber: 2g   Carbs: 9g   Protein: 26g

81. *Instant Pot Lamb Chops with Creamed Cauliflower*

Cook Time: 31 minutes   **Servings: 6**

Ingredients:

- 3 lbs. lamb chops
- 3 teaspoons sea salt
- 1 shallot, peeled, halved
- 1 cup beef stock
- 1 tablespoon tomato paste

- 2 tablespoons ghee
- 1 tablespoon extra-virgin olive oil
- 1 rosemary sprig
- Picked red onions for topping

For the Creamed Cauliflower:

- 1 head of cauliflower, cut into florets
- 3 garlic cloves, crushed
- 1 celery stalk, quartered
- 2 cups chicken stock
- Water

- 1 tablespoon unsalted butter
- ¼ cup celery leaves, chopped
- ¾ tablespoon cream
- ½ cup milk
- ½ teaspoon sea salt

Directions:

On a platter evenly distribute the rosemary leaves and salt on both sides of the lamb chops. Set your instant pot to the sauté mode, add the olive oil and butter and heat. Add the lamb chops and brown the meat on all sides for 12 minutes do chops in batches of 3. Once all the lamb chops are browned, and remove chops. Add the shallot, and tomato paste into pot stirring often. Add the beef stock. Return the lamb chops back to the pot. Cover and cook on high-pressure for 2 minutes. Once cooked use quick-release on the pressure. Meanwhile place the cauliflower, chicken stock, garlic, and celery into a pan. Add enough water to cover. Bring to a boil over medium-high heat, cook for about 15 minutes. Drain the liquid. Add cauliflower to food processor along with butter, salt, milk and cream. Puree cauliflower until it is creamy and smooth, then stir in the celery leaves.

Place the lamb chops on top of the creamed cauliflower, top with pan sauce and pickled red onions. Serve hot!

82. *Instant Pot Cooked Lamb Tagine*

Cook Time: 25 minutes   **Servings: 6**

Ingredients:

- 3 lbs. leg of lamb, diced
- 2 tablespoons ghee
- 3 teaspoons cumin, ground
- ½ teaspoon cinnamon, ground
- 2 medium onions, sliced
- 2 garlic cloves, peeled and chopped
- 1 (14-ounce can) tomatoes, chopped
- 3 tablespoons honey, organic
- 1 beef stock cube
- 1 medium sweet potato, diced
- 6 no-soak dried apricots
- 1 ½ cups water
- Garnish with parsley, fresh leaf
- Lemon zest for garnish
- 1 (15-ounce can) chickpeas, drained, rinsed

Directions:

Set your instant pot to the sauté mode, add the ghee and heat. Add the lamb, garlic, onions, and sauté, browning meat on all sides, add the spices and stir well for about 5 minutes. Add the chopped tomatoes, honey, chickpeas, sweet potato, apricots, and crumble stock cube on top. Give it a good stir and mix well. Add water. Lock the lid on the instant pot and select the Meat/Stew setting with a cook time of 15 minutes.

Release the pressure naturally, for 15 minutes. Divide into serving dishes and garnish with lemon zest and fresh parsley leaves. Serve warm.

Nutritional Information per serving:
Calories: 323 Fat: 18g Fiber: 2g Carbs: 9g Protein: 27g

83. *Lamb, Butternut Squash & Chickpea Tagine*

Cook Time: 30 minutes   **Servings: 4**

Ingredients:

- 2 lbs. lamb shoulder, cut into small chunks
- 1 (14-ounce can) chickpeas, drained, rinsed
- 1 small butternut squash, peeled, diced into small chunks
- 1 (14-ounce can) tomatoes, chopped
- 1 tablespoon coconut oil
- ½ teaspoon cinnamon, ground
- ½ teaspoon ginger, ground
- 1 teaspoon coriander, ground
- 2 teaspoons cumin, ground
- ½ teaspoon sea salt
- 1 tablespoon runny honey, organic
- 3 cloves garlic, crushed
- 1 onion, diced
- 1 cup water

Directions:

Set your instant pot to the sauté mode, add the coconut oil and heat. Add the onions and garlic, and allow to soften for 3 minutes. Now add the lamb and brown meat on all sides for another 5 minutes. Add spices and allow them to coat the meat, stir to blend.

Add tomatoes with 1 cup water and stir. Add in the honey and stir. Cancel the sauté setting. Put the lid on your instant pot and press the Manual setting with a cook time of

30 minutes. Serve with cauliflower rice or couscous with plain Greek yogurt on top and some fresh coriander, chopped. Divide into serving dishes. Serve warm.

Nutritional Information per serving:
Calories: 283 Fat: 10g Fiber: 2g Carbs: 3g Protein: 24g

84. Lamb Tagine with Orange & Prunes

Cook Time: 30 minutes   **Servings: 4**

Ingredients:

For Lamb Tagine:

- 2 lbs. lamb shoulder, cut into small pieces
- 2 teaspoons cinnamon
- 2 teaspoons turmeric
- 1 teaspoon ginger
- 2 medium onions, finely sliced
- 1 teaspoon sea salt
- ½ cup prunes
- 1 orange, peeled, and juiced
- 2 cups beef broth
- 2 garlic cloves, crushed
- 2 tablespoons ghee

For Cilantro Buttered Couscous:

- 1 large cauliflower
- ½ bunch cilantro, finely chopped
- 2 tablespoons butter
- 1 ½ teaspoons sea salt

Directions:

Add the spices to a large bowl and add the lamb meat. Mix and blend with hands to coat meat with spices then set aside. Set your instant pot to the sauté mode, add the ghee and heat. Add the garlic, and onions and sauté for 3 minutes. Add in the lamb mix to the instant pot and stir to blend ingredients. Brown the meat on all sides. Add the broth and stir. Cover the instant pot with the lid and set on Meat/Stew setting with a cook time of 30 minutes. When cooking is complete, release the pressure naturally for 15 minutes. Meanwhile cut the cauliflower into florets and place them into your food processor and pulse until the cauliflower has the consistency of large grain rice. In a pan heat the butter and add the cauliflower rice and cook for 5 minutes. Stir in the salt and add the cilantro just before serving. Serve the lamb over a bed of cilantro buttered rice. Serve warm.

Nutritional Information per serving:
Calories: 334 Fat: 25g Fiber: 1g Carbs: 11g Protein: 29g

85. Lamb, Vegetable & Lentil Soup

Cook Time: 35 minutes   **Servings: 8**

Ingredients:

- 2 lbs. lamb shanks, cut into small pieces
- 2 tablespoons coconut oil
- 2 cloves garlic, minced
- 2 carrots, chopped
- 2 celery ribs, chopped
- ½ cup peas, frozen
- 2/3 cup green lentil, rinsed, drained
- ½ cup dry white wine
- 5 cups water
- 5-ounces pancetta, chopped

Directions:

Set your instant pot to the sauté mode, add coconut oil, and heat. Add the lamb and brown the meat on all sides for about 5 minutes, then remove the meat from pot. Add the garlic, carrot, celery, pancetta, and onion into pot and sauté for about 3 minutes. Return the lamb to the pot along with wine and water, stir. Secure the lid on the pot and set on Manual setting with a cook time of 20 minutes on high pressure. When cooking is done use the quick-release to release the pressure. Add the lentils and set on Manual for a 10-minute cook time. Release pressure again using quick-release method and remove the lamb to cutting board, shred meat using 2 forks. Return the meat back to the pot along with peas. Cook for an additional 5 minutes on simmer setting. Season to taste. Pour into serving bowls. Serve hot!

Nutritional Information per serving:
Calories: 330   Fat: 25g   Fiber: 24g   Carbs: 5g   Protein: 51g

86. *Tuscan Lamb with White Beans*
Cook Time: 25 minutes   **Servings: 4**
Ingredients:

- 2 lbs. lamb shanks
- 2 tablespoons ghee
- 1 medium onion, chopped
- 3 ½ cups water
- 1 cup navy beans, dried, picked over
- 2 rosemary sprigs

- 1 (14-ounce can) tomatoes, diced in juice
- 3 garlic cloves, thinly sliced
- 2 celery ribs, chopped
- 2 carrots, chopped
- Garnish with flat-leaf parsley, extra virgin olive oil for drizzling

Directions:
Set your instant pot to the sauté mode, add the ghee and heat it. Season the lamb shanks with salt and pepper and pat dry. Add the lamb to instant pot and brown the meat on all sides. Remove the meat to a plate. Add the carrots, celery, onion, and garlic to the instant pot and sauté for about five minutes, stirring often. Add the beans, water and salt and pepper to instant pot and stir. Return the lamb shanks to the instant pot and secure the lid of pot and set on Manual setting for 30 minutes. Release the pressure naturally for 10 minutes. Place the meat on a cutting board and shred the meat using 2 forks. Spoon the beans and vegetable mixture into serving bowls and top with lamb and sauce.

Nutritional Information per serving:
Calories: 317   Fat: 22g   Fiber: 20g   Carbs: 8g   Protein: 38g

87. *Moroccan Lamb Stew*
Cook Time: 45 minutes   **Servings: 4**
Ingredients:

- 1 lb. grass-fed lamb, cubed stew meat
- 1 tablespoon coconut oil
- ½ lemon peel zested
- 1 bulb fennel cut into cubes
- ¼ cup raw almonds, toasted

- 3 tablespoons lemon juice, fresh squeezed
- ½ cup flat leaf parsley, fresh, chopped
- 20 green olives, pitted

- 2 turnips peeled, cubed
- ½ cup raisins
- 1 yellow onion, diced
- 4 carrots, peeled, sliced
- 14-ounces of pureed tomatoes
- 1 cinnamon stick
- ¼ teaspoon cloves, ground
- ¼ teaspoon cayenne
- 1 teaspoon black pepper
- Sea salt to taste
- 2 teaspoons cardamom, ground
- 1 teaspoon cumin, ground
- 2 teaspoons coriander ground
- 2 teaspoons smoked paprika
- 2 teaspoons ginger ground

Directions:

In a large container with lid, add lemon zest, coconut oil, ginger, paprika, coriander, cumin, pepper, cayenne, saffron, cinnamon stick, cardamom, and sea salt. Add the cubed lamb and mix well place lid on container and store in the fridge for 24 hours. When ready to begin cooking place the lamb mixture into your instant pot and layer the top of meat with raisins, turnips, carrots, fennel and onions. Mix the tomato puree with enough water to make 3 cups and slowly pour over meat mixture. Stir mixture. Set the lid on the instant pot and set it to the Meat/Stew setting on a cook time of 35 minutes. When the cooking is done release the pressure naturally for 15 minutes. Add the stew to serving bowls and top with chopped parsley, cilantro and toasted almonds. Serve warm.

Nutritional Information per serving:

Calories: 308   Fat: 19g   Fiber: 3g   Carbs: 9g   Protein: 29g

88. Instant Pot Rack of Lamb

Cook Time: 30 minutes   **Servings: 6**

Ingredients:

- 2 racks of lamb, about 1 lb, with about 8 ribs each
- ¼ teaspoon parsley flakes
- ¼ teaspoon black pepper
- ½ teaspoon seasoned salt
- ¼ teaspoon rosemary, ground
- ¼ teaspoon, marjoram
- ¼ teaspoon, savory
- ¼ teaspoon thyme
- ¼ cup water
- 1 tablespoon extra virgin olive oil

Directions:

Add the water to your instant pot, set racks into pot. Brush the lamb with olive oil. Mix the remaining ingredients in a small bowl. Coat the lamb with this mixture. Secure instant pot lid and set to Manual setting with a cook time of 30 minutes. When cook time is complete, release the pressure naturally for 10 minutes. Place racks on serving dishes. Serve.

Nutritional Information per serving:

Calories: 297   Fat: 15g   Fiber: 4g   Carbs: 9g   Protein: 33g

89. Garlic Rosemary Lamb

Cook Time: 25 minutes   **Servings: 6**

Ingredients:

- 1 rack of lamb
- ½ cup vegetable stock
- 4 carrots, chopped
- 4 garlic cloves, minced
- Salt and pepper to taste
- 2 tablespoons coconut oil
- 3 tablespoons coconut flour
- 4 pieces of fresh rosemary

Directions:

Season the lamb with salt and pepper. Set your instant pot to the sauté mode. Cook the lamb in instant pot along with garlic until brown on all sides for about 5 minutes. Add flour and stir. Add stock, rosemary, and carrots. Stir well. Close the lid and cook on Manual setting for 20 minutes. Once cooking is done, release the pressure naturally for 10 minutes. Remove the rosemary. Divide onto serving plates. Serve.

Nutritional Information per serving:

Calories: 287   Fat: 16g   Fiber: 9g   Carbs: 8g   Protein: 34g

---

90. Lamb Shanks with Garlic & Port Wine

Cook Time: 45 minutes   **Servings: 2**

Ingredients:

- 2 lbs. lamb shanks
- 1 tablespoon ghee
- 8 garlic cloves, peeled and left whole
- ½ cup chicken stock
- ½ cup port wine
- 1 teaspoon balsamic vinegar
- 1 tablespoon rosemary, dried
- 1 tablespoon tomato paste
- Salt and pepper to taste
- 1 tablespoon unsalted butter

Directions:

Season the lamb shanks with salt and pepper. Set the instant pot to the sauté mode, add the ghee and heat. Add the lamb shanks and brown them on all sides. Add the garlic cloves. Add the port wine, tomato paste, stock, rosemary, and stir. Close the instant pot and set on Manual setting for 30 minutes. When cooking is done release the pressure naturally for 10 minutes. Remove the lamb shanks. Set the instant pot on cook for an additional 5 minutes to thicken the sauce, add in the butter and vinegar, stir. Serve the sauce over the lamb. Serve hot!

Nutritional Information per serving:

Calories: 282   Fat: 23g   Fiber: 10g   Carbs: 9g   Protein: 36g

---

91. Instant Pot Irish Lamb Stew

Cook Time: 40 minutes   **Servings: 6**

Ingredients:

- 3 lbs. lamb shoulder, boneless, cut into small chunks
- 2 medium onions, sliced thin
- 2 medium russet potatoes, peeled, sliced 1/4 -inch thick
- 2 sprigs of thyme, fresh

- 2 cups beef broth
- ¼ cup parsley, minced

- 2 large carrots, peeled cut into 1 1/2 -inch lengths
- Sea salt and black pepper to taste

Directions:
In a vegetable basket that will fit into your instant pot, place the potatoes, carrots, parsley, with a pinch of salt and pepper and set aside. Layer the rest of the ingredients in the instant pot with salt and pepper. Add in the beef stock pouring over everything. Then place the basket on top of them. Set the instant pot to Manual setting for 20 minutes. Now set the pot at high pressure for 20 minutes. Release the pressure naturally for 15 minutes. Remove the basket of vegetables from pot and set on a plate. Remove the thyme sprigs from stew. Add the vegetables in the basket back into instant pot and stir the stew. Add more sea salt and black pepper as needed. Divide into serving bowls. Serve hot!

Nutritional Information per serving:
Calories: 256   Fat: 16g   Fiber: 14g   Carbs: 7g   Protein: 35g

92. *Instant Pot Lamb Stew Provencal*
Cook Time: 45 minutes   **Servings: 4**
Ingredients:
- ¾ cup coconut flour
- 1 lb. lamb stew meat, cubed
- 2 tablespoons coconut oil
- 1 shallot, finely chopped
- 1 cup red wine
- 1 teaspoon garlic, minced
- 4 cups beef stock
- 1-inch rosemary

- 2 bay leaves
- 1 cup pearl onions
- 1 tablespoon Herbes de Provence
- 2 cups mushrooms quartered
- 4 cups vegetable roots, cubed
- Sea salt and black pepper to taste
- Flat leaf parsley for garnish

Directions:
Add the salt, pepper and coconut flour to a zip bag. Add the cubed lamb to bag and zip the top. Shake until the pieces of meat are coated. Set your instant pot to the sauté mode, add the coconut oil and heat it up. Shake excess coating off meat and place the meat into the instant pot along with shallot and garlic.

Stir until the meat is browned on all sides, for about 5 minutes. Add the beef stock and red wine to the instant pot along with bay leaves, rosemary, and Herbes de Provence, and stir to combine. Set to Meat/Stew setting for 30 minutes. When cooking is complete, release the pressure naturally in 15 minutes. While your lamb is cooking, prep your vegetables. Blanch the pearl onions quickly, snip the root end, and pop the onion out of its skin. Add the vegetables to the instant pot, and cook on Manual setting for 10 minutes. Release the pressure again with quick-release. Divide into serving bowls, and garnish with parsley. Serve hot!

Nutritional Information per serving:
Calories: 572   Fat: 46g   Fiber: 10g   Carbs: 4.2g   Protein: 31g

93. Guinness Lamb Stew with Vegetables
Cook Time: 40 minutes   **Servings: 6**
Ingredients:

- 3 lbs. lamb shoulder, cut into small pieces
- 3 tablespoons coconut oil
- 2 medium yellow onions, sliced thin
- 6 cloves garlic, peeled, smashed
- 1 cup frozen peas
- 6 small white potato, cut in half
- 2 teaspoons honey, organic
- 1 sprig rosemary, fresh
- 1 bay leaf
- 1/2 cup water
- 1 cups beef broth
- 1/2 cup Guinness
- 3 tablespoons tomato paste
- ¼ cup coconut flour

Directions:
Pat the lamb dry and season it with salt and pepper. Set your instant pot to sauté mode, add the coconut oil and heat. Add the onions, and garlic and stir for about 3 minutes. Add in the lamb and brown the meat on all sides for about 5 minutes, then remove the lamb from pot. Stir in the tomato paste and cook for another 3 minutes.
Add the lamb and flour back into pot, and stir. Add the water, beef broth, bay leaf, honey, rosemary sprig, and Guinness, stir. Set to Manual setting for 20 minutes and cook. When cooking is completed, release pressure naturally for 10-minutes. Add the carrots and potatoes to the stew and place the lid back on the instant pot and set on Meat/Stew setting for 20 minutes. Release pressure again when cooking is complete, and remove rosemary sprig, and bay leaf. Add the frozen peas and keep the pot on simmer for about 5 minutes. Divide into serving bowls. Serve hot!
Nutritional Information per serving:
Calories: 789 Fat: 52g Fiber: 6g Carbs: 3.6g Protein: 42g

94. Mushroom, Potato Lamb Stew
Total Cook Time: 40 minutes   **Servings: 4**
Ingredients:

- 2 lbs. lamb stew meat, cubed
- 1 large onion, chopped
- 2 tablespoons ghee
- 4 potatoes, quartered
- 2 cloves garlic, crushed
- ¼ of 14-ounce can of tomatoes, crushed
- ¼ can of button mushrooms, sliced
- Flat-leaf parsley, chopped for garnish
- Sea salt and black pepper to taste
- 2 cups beef broth

Directions:
Set your instant pot to the sauté mode, add the ghee and heat. Add the lamb with sea salt and pepper, brown meat on all sides for about 5-minutes, remove meat from pot. Add garlic and onions into the instant pot and cook for about 5-minutes stir occasionally. Add the tomato, broth, potatoes, mushrooms and the lamb back into your instant pot. Place the lid on the pot and set on Meat/Stew setting for 30 minutes. Release the pressure naturally for 15 minutes. Divide into serving bowls, and garnish with parsley. Serve hot!
Nutritional Information per serving:
Calories: 682 Fat: 51g Fiber: 10g Carbs: 3.9g Protein: 42g

95. Greek Lamb Stew with Green Beans
Cook Time: 40 minutes   **Servings: 6**
Ingredients:

- 3 lbs. leg of lamb, boneless
- 1 medium onion, finely chopped
- 1 ½ cups water
- 2 tablespoons coconut oil
- 1 lb. of string green beans, fresh, trimmed
- 3 large tomatoes, pulped in blender
- 4 tablespoons tomato sauce
- 5 potatoes, peeled and cut into small chunks
- 1 tablespoon dill, fresh, chopped
- ½ tablespoon mint, fresh chopped
- A pinch of cinnamon, ground

Directions:

Set your instant pot to the sauté mode, add the coconut oil and heat. Add the lamb and brown on sides of the meat, for about five minutes, then remove the meat from the pot. Add the onions to pot and cook for about 5-minutes stirring often. Add in the tomatoes, tomato sauce and some sea salt and stir. Add the meat back into the pot, along with the rest of the ingredients except for parsley, and stir. Cover with lid and set the pot on Meat/Stew setting for 30-minutes. Release the pressure naturally for 10-minutes. Divide into serving bowls, garnish with chopped parsley. Serve hot!

Nutritional Information per serving:

Calories: 589   Fat: 41g   Fiber: 10g   Carbs: 9g   Protein: 46g

96. Ground Lamb with Zucchini Pasta
Cook Time: 45 minutes   **Servings: 6**
Ingredients:

- 1 lb. lamb, ground
- 2 tablespoons ghee
- 1 medium white onion, finely chopped
- 2 cups chicken broth
- 1 bay leaf
- 2 stalks celery, chopped
- ½ cup water
- 1 (14-ounce can) tomatoes, crushed
- Sea salt and black pepper to taste
- 1 ½ cups of zucchini pasta
- 1 bunch of parsley, fresh, chopped for garnish

Directions:

Set your instant pot on the sauté mode, add the ghee and heat. Add the white onion and cook for 5-minutes while stirring. Add the ground lamb and cook for an additional 5-minutes. Once meat is browned transfer to a colander and drain. Add the tomatoes, water, broth, celery, bay leaf, sea salt and pepper. Set the instant pot to the Meat/Stew setting for 35-minutes. When cooking is completed, release the pressure naturally for 10-minutes. Divide into serving bowls, serve on top of bed of zucchini pasta, and garnish with parsley. Serve hot!

Nutritional Information per serving:

Calories: 623   Fat: 46g   Fiber: 13g   Carbs: 12g   Protein: 42g

97. Greek Lamb Shanks with Tomatoes

Cooking time: 50 minutes   **Servings: 4**

Ingredients:

- 4 lamb shanks
- 2 tablespoons extra-virgin olive oil
- 1 (14-ounce can) tomatoes, crushed
- 1 cup chicken stock
- ½ cup red wine
- ¼ teaspoon cinnamon, ground
- 1 teaspoon, thyme, dried
- 1 teaspoon, oregano, dried
- 1 tablespoon, tomato paste
- 4 cloves garlic, crushed
- 1 carrot, peeled, minced
- 1 stalk of celery, minced
- 1 large onion, minced
- Sea salt and black pepper to taste

Directions:

Set your instant pot to the sauté mode, add the oil and heat it up. Add the shanks and brown the meat on all sides, 3-minutes on each side, then remove the shanks from pot. Add the onion, celery, and carrot to food processor and process until minced. Add the minced vegetables to your instant pot, along with stock, wine, spices, and lamb shanks, stir well. Secure the lid and set the instant pot onto the Meat/Stew setting for 30 minutes. When cooking is completed, release the pressure for 15 minutes naturally. Divide the into serving dishes, drizzle sauce over from instant pot. Serve hot!

Nutritional Information per serving:

Calories: 641   Fat: 48g   Fiber: 16g   Carbs: 13g   Protein: 44g

98. Lamb & White Bean Stew

Cook Time: 50 minutes   **Servings: 4**

Ingredients:

- 2 ½ lbs. lamb shoulder, boneless, cubed
- 1 ½ cups white beans, dried
- 2 tablespoons ghee
- 2 bay leaves
- 2 onions, cut into rings
- ½ bunch parsley, fresh, chopped
- 1 large tomato, diced
- 2 tablespoons curry powder
- 2 bunches spring onion, chopped, set aside 2 tablespoons for garnish
- 2 garlic cloves, chopped
- Pinch of cayenne pepper
- 1 teaspoon cumin, ground
- 2 cups chicken stock

Directions:

Soak the white beans overnight in 2 cups cold water. When ready to cook, set your instant pot to the sauté mode, add the ghee and heat. Add the lamb and brown the meat on all sides. Add the onion, garlic, cayenne pepper, cumin, curry powder, salt and pepper, cook for 5 minutes, stirring. Drain the beans and remaining ingredients, except for 2 tablespoons of chopped green onion, then add them to your instant pot along with stock and stir. Put on the lid to instant pot and set it on the Meat/Stew setting 35 minutes. When the cooking is complete, release the pressure for 10-minutes. Divide into serving bowls, and top with chopped spring onion. Serve hot!

Nutritional Information per serving:

Calories: 633   Fat: 49g   Fiber: 10g   Carbs: 12g   Protein: 49g

99. Lamb Trotters with Tomato & Thyme
Cooking Time: 50 minutes
Servings: 4
Ingredients:

- 2 lbs lamb trotters
- 4 cloves of garlic, chopped
- 2 medium white onions, chopped
- 1 chive, chopped
- 3 bay leaves
- 2 carrots, peeled, sliced
- 12 peppercorns
- 1 cup white wine
- 3 chilli peppers
- 1 cup tomato puree
- 1 tablespoon thyme, fresh, chopped
- Sea salt and black pepper to taste
- ½ cup water
- 1 tablespoon olive oil

Directions:
Wash the lamb trotters under cold running water. Set your instant pot to the sauté mode, add the oil and heat. Add the onions, and garlic and sauté for 5 minutes. Place the trotters into your instant pot, along with wine, water, bay leaves, peppercorns, tomato puree and remaining spices, except the thyme. Set the instant pot to the Manual setting for 45 minutes. When cooking is complete, release the pressure for 15 minutes naturally. Divide into servings dishes, and garnish with fresh, chopped thyme. Serve hot!

Nutritional Information per serving:
Calories: 1290   Fat: 53g   Fiber: 28g   Carbs: 14g   Protein: 64g

---

100. Mensaf (Jordanian Lamb Stew)
Cook Time: 45 minutes
Servings: 8
Ingredients:

- 2 lbs. lamb shoulder, boneless, cubed
- ¼ cup pinenuts
- 1 cups chicken stock
- ½ cup white wine
- 2 cup goat's milk
- 2 tablespoons coconut oil
- Serve with cauliflower rice
- Pita bread for serving

Directions:
Set your instant pot to the sauté mode, add the coconut oil and heat. Add the lamb and brown the meat on all sides for about 5-minutes, then remove meat from pot. Add the pinenuts and toast them for 3-minutes, then remove them. Add in the wine, stock, goats milk and stir. Cook on Manual setting with a cook time of 40-minutes. When cooking is completed, release the pressure naturally in 10-minutes. Stir the stew pour over bed of cauliflower rice that is on top of piece of pita bread. Garnish with toasted pinenuts. Serve hot!

Nutritional Information per serving:
Calories: 642   Fat: 49g   Fiber: 10g   Carbs: 13g   Protein: 47g

Chapter 6. Poultry Instant Pot Recipes

101. *Garlic Chicken*

Cook Time: 35 minutes   **Servings: 8**

Ingredients:

- 2 lbs. chicken thighs, skinless, boneless
- 1 cup Parmesan cheese, grated
- 8-ounces cream cheese
- 1 cup chicken broth
- 1 teaspoon black pepper, freshly ground
- 2 teaspoons sea salt
- 2 teaspoons paprika
- 8 garlic cloves, minced
- 1 onion, diced
- 12-ounces cremini mushrooms or button mushrooms, halved
- ½ cup unsalted butter, melted
- Parsley, fresh for garnish

Directions:

Place your chicken thighs into your instant pot, and pour the melted butter over the chicken. Add the onion, garlic, mushrooms, salt and pepper, toss to coat the chicken thighs with butter. Cover and set on the Meat/Stew setting for 35 minutes.

Once the cooking is completed, release the pressure naturally for 15 minutes. Remove the chicken and vegetables to a serving platter. Set your instant pot to the sauté mode for 5 minutes. Combine the chicken broth, with Parmesan cheese and cream cheese. Cook, stirring, mixture until the cream cheese is fully melted. Pour the sauce over your chicken thighs and garnish with fresh parsley. Serve hot!

Nutritional Information per serving:

Calories: 495   Fat: 41g   Carbs: 6g   Protein: 26g

102. *Ground Turkey & Basil Meatballs*

Cook Time: 40 minutes   **Servings: 8**

Ingredients:

For the Sauce:

- 1 teaspoon parsley, dried
- 2 teaspoons basil, dried
- 2 garlic cloves, minced
- 1 tablespoon extra-virgin olive oil

For the Meatballs:

- 2 large eggs
- 2 cups cauliflower rice
- ½ teaspoon garlic powder
- ½ teaspoon black pepper, freshly ground
- 1 teaspoon sea salt
- 1 tablespoon Italian seasoning
- 2 cups Parmesan cheese, grated, divided

- 1 (14-ounce can) tomatoes, crushed
- ½ stick of unsalted butter
- 1 cup heavy whipping cream
- Sea salt and black pepper to taste

- ½ cup almond meal
- 12-ounces ground turkey
- 1 lb. Italian sausage, casings removed
- 8-ounces fontina cheese, cut into 24 cubes
- 2 tablespoons coconut oil

Directions:

In a mixing bowl, beat the eggs, then whisk in the almond meal, cauliflower rice, Italian seasoning, 1 cup Parmesan cheese, salt, pepper, and garlic powder. Add the sausage and turkey and mix to combine. Form 24 (1-inch) balls. In the center of each meatball stuff a fontina cheese cube, making sure the cheese is fully encased. Place the stuffed meatballs into your instant pot. Set your instant pot to the sauté mode, and add the coconut oil and heat it. Add the meatballs to the melted coconut oil, and brown them on all sides for 5 minutes. Add in the remaining ingredients to instant pot, except the heavy whipping cream, stir and place the lid securely onto instant pot. Set the instant pot to the Meat/Stew setting for a cook time of 30 minutes. When cooking is completed, release the pressure naturally for 15 minutes. Remove the meatballs from instant pot, and add the cream into the sauce in the instant pot and stir to blend. Add the meatballs back into the pot and set to the Keep Warm/Cancel setting until ready to serve. Serve hot!

Nutritional Information per serving:
Calories: 633   Fat: 50g   Carbs: 9g   Protein: 39g

---

103. *Creamy Mushroom, Rosemary Chicken*
Cook Time: 45 minutes   **Servings: 6**
Ingredients:

- 2 lbs. chicken breasts, skinless, boneless
- 8-ounces bacon, diced
- 8-ounces button mushrooms, halved
- 1 cup sour cream
- Sea salt and black pepper to taste
- 3 fresh rosemary sprigs
- 6 garlic cloves, minced
- ½ cup dry white wine
- ½ stick butter, cubed
- 2 tablespoons coconut oil
- Fresh parsley, chopped for garnish

Directions:
Set your instant pot to the sauté mode, add the coconut oil and heat. Add the diced bacon to instant pot and cook until semi-crispy. Add the chicken and brown the meat for about five minutes. Add in the wine to instant pot and stir mixture. Add in the remaining ingredients, except for parsley, stir and secure the lid of instant pot. Set to the Meat/Stew setting for 35 minutes. When the cooking is complete, release pressure naturally for 10-minutes. Remove the rosemary sprigs and discard. Divide among serving dishes. Garnish with fresh chopped parsley. Serve hot!

Nutritional Information per serving:
Calories: 570   Fat: 49g   Carbs: 5g   Protein: 27g

---

104. *Heavy Cream Chicken Stew*
Cook Time: 40 minutes   **Servings: 4**
Ingredients:

- 12-ounces whole chicken thighs and legs
- ¼ cup extra-virgin olive oil
- 1 teaspoon fennel seeds, crushed
- 1 tablespoon tomato paste
- 2 tablespoons dry white wine
- 2 garlic cloves, minced
- ½ onion, diced
- 1 stalk celery, chopped
- 1 cup black olives, pitted
- 1 cup chicken broth

- 1 cup heavy whipping cream
- 2 tablespoons fresh chopped parsley for garnish
- Sea salt and black pepper to taste

Directions:

Place the chicken broth, olives, celery, garlic, onion, white wine, tomato paste, fennel seeds, sea salt, black pepper, stir, then add in chicken pieces, and stir. Cover instant pot and set to Meat/Stew setting for 45 minutes. When the cooking is completed, release the pressure naturally for 15-minutes. Add in the heavy cream and stir. Divide into serving bowls, and garnish with fresh chopped parsley. Serve hot.

Nutritional Information per serving:

Calories: 447   Fat: 34g   Carbs: 7g   Protein: 26g

---

105. Ginger Spinach Chicken

Cook Time: 50 minutes   **Servings: 8**

Ingredients:

- 1 tablespoon ginger, minced
- 8 chicken thighs
- 2 cups baby spinach
- 1 teaspoon blackstrap molasses
- 1 tablespoon garlic powder
- 2 cups chicken stock
- Sea salt and black pepper to taste
- Chopped coriander, fresh, for garnish

Directions:

Add the chicken stock, salt, pepper, ginger, garlic powder, and mix, then add in the chicken thighs. Set the instant pot to Meat/Stew setting for a cook time of 45 minutes. When cook time is completed, release pressure within 10-minutes naturally. Add the spinach to the instant pot and stir, set on Manual for 5-minute cook time. Divide into serving dishes, and garnish with fresh, chopped coriander. Serve hot!

Nutritional Information per serving:

Calories: 472   Fat: 35g   Carbs: 3.8g   Protein: 32.7g

---

106. Ginger Coconut Chicken Wings

Cook Time: 50 minutes   **Servings: 6**

Ingredients:

- 3 lbs. chicken wings
- 8-ounces curry paste
- 2-ounces Thai basil, minced
- 1 tablespoon coconut milk
- 1 tablespoon ginger, fresh, minced
- 1 tablespoon cilantro, fresh, minced

Directions:

Add your chicken wings into your instant pot. In a mixing bowl, whisk together cilantro, coconut milk, ginger, curry paste and basil. Pour the milk mixture over your chicken wings and toss to coat. Cover and cook on Meat/Stew setting for 50 minutes. When the cook time is complete, release the pressure naturally within 15-minutes. Remove lid and stir. Divide into serving dishes, and serve hot!

Nutritional Information per serving:

Calories: 332   Fat: 14.3g   Carbs: 6.3g   Protein: 39.6g

107. Spicy, Creamy, Coconut Chicken
Cook Time: 40 minutes   **Servings: 5**
Ingredients:

- 1 lb. chicken thighs, boneless, skinless
- 2 tablespoons olive oil
- 2 teaspoons onion powder
- 3 garlic cloves, minced
- 1 tablespoon ginger, grated
- 3 tablespoons tomato paste
- 5 teaspoons garam masala
- 2 teaspoons paprika
- 10-ounces tomatoes, diced
- 1 cup heavy cream
- 1 cup coconut milk

Directions:
Cut the chicken up into pieces, and add to your instant pot. Add the grated ginger on top of the chicken pieces, then add the rest of the spices. Add the tomato paste, and tomatoes, along with olive oil, and mix well. Add half a cup of coconut milk and stir well. Secure the lid and set the instant pot on the Meat/Stew setting for 35 minutes. When the cook time is complete, release the pressure naturally for 10-minutes. Add to instant pot the heavy cream, and remaining coconut milk, stir. Replace the lid and set on Manual for 5-minutes of cook time. Divide into serving dishes. Serve hot!

Nutritional Information per serving:
Calories: 444   Fat: 33g   Carbs: 10g   Protein: 29.2g

---

108. Jalapeno, Curry, Garlic Chicken Meatballs
Cook Time: 45 minutes   **Servings: 3**
Ingredients:

- 1 lb. lean ground chicken
- 2 cloves garlic, minced, divided
- 1 tablespoon ginger, fresh, minced, divided
- 2 green onions, chopped
- 1 tablespoon cilantro, fresh, chopped
- ½ cup chicken broth
- 1 tablespoon basil, fresh, chopped
- 2 tablespoons almond meal
- 1 jalapeno, sliced
- 1 cup light coconut milk
- 2 tablespoons Thai green curry paste, divided
- Sea salt and black pepper to taste
- 2 tablespoons coconut oil

Directions:
Add to a mixing bowl, the ground chicken, green onion, cilantro, basil, almond meal, half the ginger, garlic, Thai curry paste, salt and pepper, and mix well. Divide the mixture into 12 equal portions and shape into balls. Add the rest of the ingredients into your instant pot, and mix well. Set your instant pot onto the sauté mode, add the coconut oil and heat. Add the balls into the instant pot.
Brown the meatballs for about 5-minutes, then remove the meatballs from instant pot. Add the rest of the ingredients into the instant pot and stir to combine. Add the meatballs, carefully back into the instant pot. Secure the lid and place on Meat/Stew setting on a cook time of 40 minutes. When the cook time is complete, release the pressure naturally for 15-minutes. Divide into serving dishes, and serve hot!

Nutritional Information per serving:
Calories: 284   Fat: 15g   Carbs: 3g   Protein: 33g

109. Chicken Breasts & Spicy Sauce

Cook Time: 25 minutes   **Servings: 4**

Ingredients:

- 2 chicken breasts, skinless, boneless, chopped
- ¼ teaspoon ginger, grated
- 1 tablespoon garam masala
- 1 cup Greek yogurt, plain
- 1 tablespoon lemon juice
- Sea salt and black pepper to taste

For the Sauce:

- ¼ teaspoon cayenne
- ½ teaspoon turmeric
- ½ teaspoon paprika
- 15-ounce can of tomato sauce
- 4 garlic cloves, minced
- 4 teaspoons garam masala

Directions:

In a mixing bowl, add lemon juice, chicken, yogurt, 1 tablespoon garam masala, ginger, salt, pepper, and toss well, then leave in the fridge for an hour. Set your instant pot to the sauté mode, add the chicken, and stir and cook for 5-minutes. Add 4 teaspoons garam masala, paprika, turmeric, cayenne, tomato sauce, stir and cover. Set the instant pot to the Meat/Stew setting on a high cook time of 20 minutes. Once the cook time is complete, release the pressure naturally for 20 minutes. Divide between serving plates. Serve hot!

Nutritional Information per serving:

Calories: 452   Fat: 4g   Fiber: 7g   Carbs: 9g   Protein: 12g

110. Chicken & Spaghetti Squash

Cook Time: 20 minutes   **Servings: 4**

Ingredients:

- 1 spaghetti squash, halved, seedless
- 1 lb. chicken, cooked, cubed
- 16-ounces Mozzarella cheese, shredded
- 1 cup water
- 1 cup keto marinara sauce

Directions:

Place a cup of water into your instant pot, add the trivet, add the squash, cover and cook on Manual setting on high for a 20-minute cook time. Shred squash and transfer it into a heatproof bowl. Add the marinara sauce, chicken, and mozzarella, toss. Add the squash back into the instant pot, along with marinara sauce, chicken, and mozzarella, stir and close the lid. Set to Manual setting for 5-minutes. Divide into serving bowls. Serve warm!

Nutritional Information per serving:

Calories: 329   Fat: 6g   Fiber: 6   Carbs: 9g   Protein: 10g

111. Chicken & Cauliflower Rice

Cook Time: 38 minutes   **Servings: 6**

Ingredients:

- 3 lbs. chicken thighs, boneless, skinless
- 3 carrots, chopped
- 3 bacon slices, chopped
- 1 rhubarb stalk, chopped

- 4 garlic cloves, minced
- ¼ cup red wine vinegar
- 2 bay leaves
- 1 cup beef stock
- 1 teaspoon turmeric powder
- 24-ounces cauliflower rice
- 1 tablespoon Italian seasoning
- 1 tablespoon garlic powder
- ¼ cup olive oil
- Sea salt and black pepper to taste

Directions:

Set your instant pot on the sauté mode, add the oil and heat. Add bacon, onion, rhubarb, carrots, and garlic, cook for 8 minutes. Add the chicken and stir for 5 minutes. Add the vinegar, turmeric, Italian seasoning, bay leaves, and garlic powder, stir. Cover with lid and set to Meat/Stew setting and cook on high for 20-minutes. When cooking is complete, release the pressure naturally in 15-minutes. Add the cauliflower rice to instant pot with beef stock, stir, cover, and set on Manual setting and cook on low for 5-minutes. Divide into serving bowls. Serve warm!

Nutritional Information per serving:

Calories: 310 Fat: 16g Fiber: 3g Carbs: 6g Protein: 10g

112. *Chicken Curry*

Cook Time: 30 minutes   **Servings: 4**

Ingredients:

- 2lbs. chicken thighs, skinless, boneless, and cubed
- 3 tomatoes, chopped
- 1 tablespoon water
- 3 red chilies, chopped
- 1 cup white onion, chopped
- 2 garlic cloves, minced
- 14-ounces canned, coconut milk
- 1 cup chicken stock
- 2 tablespoons coconut oil
- 1 tablespoon lime juice
- 1 teaspoon fennel seeds, ground
- 1 teaspoon cumin, ground
- 1 teaspoon turmeric, ground
- 1 teaspoon cinnamon, ground
- 2 teaspoons coriander, ground
- 1 tablespoon ginger, grated
- Sea salt and black pepper to taste

Directions:

In your food processor, mix the garlic, white onion, water, ginger, chilies, coriander, cinnamon, cumin, fennel, turmeric, black pepper, and blend until you have a paste and transfer it to a bowl.

Set your instant pot to the sauté mode, add the coconut oil, and heat. Add the mixed paste and stir and cook for 30 seconds. Add tomatoes, chicken, stock, stir and blend well. Cover and cook on Manual setting on high for 15-minutes. Add the coconut milk and stir mixture in pot. Cover the instant pot again and set on high for an additional 10-minutes more. Add in the lime juice, sea salt and black pepper and divide into serving bowls. Serve warm!

Nutritional Information per serving:

Calories: 430 Fat: 16g Fiber: 4 Carbs: 7g Protein: 38g

113. Chicken and Mushrooms
Cooking Time: *15 minutes*
Servings: *4*
Ingredients:

- 4 chicken thighs
- 2 cups button mushrooms, sliced
- 1 teaspoon Dijon mustard
- ½ cup water
- ½ teaspoon garlic powder
- Sea salt and black pepper to taste
- ¼ cup of ghee
- 1 tablespoon tarragon, chopped
- ½ teaspoon onion, powder

Directions:
Set your instant pot to the saute mode, add the ghee and heat it. Add the chicken thighs, onion powder, garlic powder, salt, pepper, and stir. Cook chicken on each side for 2 minutes, then transfer to a bowl. Add the mushrooms into your instant pot, stir and sauté them for 2 minutes. Return the chicken to your instant pot, add the mustard, water, and stir well, cover and cook on high for 10 minutes on Manual setting. When cooking is completed, release the pressure naturally, for 10-minutes. Add the tarragon and stir, divide between serving plates. Serve warm!
Nutritional Information per serving:
Calories: 263   Fat: 16g   Fiber: 4g   Carbs: 6g   Protein: 18g

114. Chicken and Salsa
Cook Time: *17 minutes*
Servings: *6*
Ingredients:

- 6 chicken breasts, skinless, boneless
- 2 tablespoons of olive oil
- 1 cup cheddar cheese, shredded
- Sea salt and black pepper to taste
- 2 cups jarred keto salsa

Directions:
Set your instant pot on sauté mode, add the oil and heat. Add the chicken, stir and cook for 2 minutes on each side. Add the salsa, stir, cover and cook on high on Manual setting. When cooking is completed, release the pressure naturally for 10 minutes. Spread the cheese over top of mix in the instant pot. Cook again for an additional 3 minutes more on high setting. Divide between serving plates. Serve warm!
Nutritional Information per serving:
Calories: 220   Fat: 17g   Fiber: 2g   Carbs: 6g   Protein: 12g

115. Chicken, Walnuts, and Pomegranate

Cook Time: 17 minutes　　　　　　　**Servings: 6**

Ingredients:

- 12 chicken thighs
- 3 tablespoons coconut oil
- 2 cups walnuts, toasted, chopped
- 1 yellow onion, chopped
- Juice of ½ a lemon
- ¼ teaspoon cardamom, ground
- ½ teaspoon cinnamon, ground
- 1 cup pomegranate molasses
- 2 tablespoons Truvia

Directions:

Place the walnuts in your food processor, blend and transfer to a bowl. Set your instant pot to the sauté mode, add the oil and heat it up. Add the chicken, salt and pepper and brown for 3-minutes on each side, transfer chicken to a bowl. Add the onion, walnuts, and sauté for 2-minutes. Add the pomegranate molasses, cardamom, lemon juice, chicken, Truvia and stir. Cover and set to Manual cooking on high for 12 minutes. When cooking is completed, release the pressure naturally for 15-minutes. Divide amongst serving plates. Serve hot!

Nutritional Information per serving:

Calories: 265　Fat: 16g　Fiber: 6g　Carbs: 6g　Protein: 16g

---

116. Turkey Instant Pot Stew

Cook Time: 33 minutes　　　　　　　**Servings: 4**

Ingredients:

- 2 tablespoons avocado oil
- 3 cups turkey meat, cooked, shredded
- Sea salt and black pepper to taste
- 2 carrots, chopped
- 3 celery stalks, chopped
- 1 teaspoon garlic, minced
- 1 yellow onion, chopped
- 1 tablespoon cranberry sauce
- 5 cups turkey stock
- 15-ounce can of tomatoes, chopped

Directions:

Set your instant pot to the sauté mode, add the oil and heat it up. Add the celery, carrots, and onions, stir and cook for 3-minutes. Add the cranberry sauce, stock, garlic, turkey meat, salt and pepper, stir, cover. Cook on Manual setting on low for 30-minutes. When cooking is completed, release the pressure for 15-minutes. Divide into serving bowls. Serve hot!

Nutritional Information per serving:

Calories: 200　Fat: 14g　Fiber: 1g　Carbs: 6g　Protein: 16g

---

117. Lemongrass Chicken

Cook Time: 20 minutes　　　　　　　**Servings: 5**

Ingredients:

- 1 bunch lemongrass, bottom removed and trimmed
- 1-inch piece ginger root, peeled and chopped

- 4-garlic cloves, peeled and crushed
- 1 tablespoon lime juice
- 1 yellow onion, chopped
- ¼ cup cilantro, diced
- 2 tablespoons coconut oil
- Sea salt and black pepper to taste
- 10-chicken drumsticks
- 2 tablespoons fish sauce

Directions:

In your food processor mix the lemongrass, with the garlic, ginger, fish sauce, five spice powder and pulse well. Add the coconut milk and pulse again. Set your instant pot to the sauté mode, add the coconut oil and heat it. Add the onion, stir and cook for 5-minutes. Add the chicken, salt and pepper, stir and cook for 3-minutes per side of chicken. Add the coconut milk, lemongrass mix, stir, cover. Set on the Poultry mode, and cook for 15-minutes. Release the pressure for 10-minutes naturally. Add lime juice, more salt and pepper and stir. Divide into serving plates. Serve warm!

Nutritional Information per serving:

Calories: 400   Fat: 18g   Fiber: 2g   Carbs: 6g   Protein: 20g

118. Chicken and Cabbage

Cook Time: 30 minutes   **Servings: 3**

Ingredients:

- 1 ½ lbs. chicken thighs, boneless
- 1 green cabbage, roughly chopped
- 1 yellow onion, chopped
- 2 chili peppers, chopped
- Sea salt and black pepper to taste
- 2 tablespoons ghee
- 1 tablespoon fish sauce
- 10-ounces coconut milk
- ½ cup white wine
- Cayenne pepper to taste
- 1 tablespoon curry
- 4 garlic cloves, peeled and chopped

Directions:

Set your instant pot to the sauté mode, add the ghee and heat it. Add the chicken, salt, pepper and brown on the sides of meat for about 5-minutes, then transfer chicken to a bowl. Add the chili peppers, onions, garlic to the instant pot and stir, cook for 3-minutes. Add the curry and cook for an additional 2-minutes, stirring. Add the coconut milk, wine, cabbage, fish sauce, salt, pepper, chicken, stir and cover, set to Poultry setting for 20 minutes. Release the pressure naturally, for 15-minutes. Stir and divide into serving plates. Serve hot!

Nutritional Information per serving:

Calories: 260   Fat: 25.5g   Fiber: 4.9g   Carbs: 15.2g   Protein: 30.2g

119. Chicken and Corn

Cook Time: 25 minutes   **Servings: 4**

Ingredients:

- 8-chicken drumsticks
- 2 tablespoons extra virgin olive oil
- ¼ cup cilantro, fresh, chopped
- 1 tomato, cored, chopped
- ½ yellow onion, peeled, chopped
- 3 scallions, chopped
- ½ teaspoon garlic powder
- ½ teaspoon cumin

- 2 corns on the cob, husked and cut into halves
- 1 tablespoon chicken bouillon
- 8-ounces tomato sauce
- 2 cups water
- 1 garlic clove, minced

Directions:

Set your instant pot on the sauté mode, add the oil and heat it up. Add the scallions, tomato, onions, garlic, stir and cook for 3-minutes. Add the cilantro, stir and cook for another 1-minute. Add the tomato sauce, water, bouillon, garlic powder, cumin, chicken, salt, pepper, top with corn. Cover the instant pot and cook on Poultry setting for 20-minutes. Release the pressure naturally for 15-minutes. Divide among serving plates. Serve warm!

Nutritional Information per serving:

Calories: 320   Fat: 10g   Fiber: 3g   Carbs: 1.8g   Protein: 42g

---

120. Duck Chili

Cook Time: 1 hour   **Servings: 4**

Ingredients:

- 1lb. northern beans, soaked and rinsed
- 5 cups water
- 2 cloves

For the Duck:

- 1 lb. duck, ground
- 1 tablespoon olive oil
- 1 yellow onion, minced
- ½ cup cilantro, fresh, chopped for garnish

- 1 bay leaf
- Sea salt and black pepper to taste
- 1 garlic head, top trimmed off
- 1 yellow onion, cut in half

- 15-ounces can of tomatoes, diced
- 1 teaspoon brown sugar
- 4-ounces canned green chilies
- Sea salt and black pepper to taste
- 2 carrots, chopped

Directions:

Set your instant pot to the sauté mode, add the oil, add carrots, chopped onion, season with salt and pepper and cook for 5-minutes, then transfer to a bowl. Add the duck and stir and cook for 5-minutes, transfer to a bowl. Put the beans into the instant pot, add the garlic head, onion halves, bay leaf, cloves, water, salt and stir, cover and cook on the Bean/Chili setting for 25-minutes. Release the pressure naturally for 10-minutes. Add back into the instant pot the duck, carrots, onions, tomatoes, chilies, stir. Cook on high on Manual setting for 5-minutes. Release the pressure again naturally for 10-minutes. Add into the instant pot the beans and brown sugar, stir. Add to serving bowls and garnish with fresh chopped cilantro. Serve warm!

Nutritional Information per serving:

Calories: 270   Fat: 33g   Fiber: 26g   Carbs: 15g   Protein: 25g

121. Chicken Gumbo

Cook Time: 45 minutes   **Servings: 4**

Ingredients:

- 1 lb. smoked sausage, sliced
- 1 lb. chicken thighs, cut into halves

For the Roux:

- ½ cup almond flour
- ¼ olive oil

Aromatics:

- 1 bell pepper, seeded, chopped
- Tabasco sauce
- 1 yellow onion, chopped
- 1 celery stalk, chopped
- ½ lb. okra

For Serving:

- ½ cup parsley, fresh, chopped

- 2 tablespoon olive oil, divided
- Sea salt and black pepper to taste

- 1 teaspoon Cajun spice

- 15-ounce can of tomatoes, chopped
- 2 cups chicken stock
- 4 garlic cloves, minced
- 1 carrot, peeled, sliced

- Cauliflower rice, already cooked

Directions:

Set your instant pot on the sauté mode, add 1 tablespoon oil and heat it. Add the sausage, stir and brown meat for 4-minutes, then transfer sausage to a plate. Add the chicken pieces, stir, brown chicken for 6-minutes, then transfer to a bowl. Add the remaining tablespoon of oil to the instant pot and heat it up. Add the Cajun spice to instant pot, stir and cook for 5-minutes. Add the onion, bell pepper, carrot, celery, garlic, salt, pepper and stir and cook for an additional 5-minutes. Return the chicken and sausage to the instant pot and stir, adding in the stock and tomatoes. Cover the instant pot and cook on the Meat/Stew setting for 10-minutes. Release the pressure naturally for 10-minutes. Divide into serving bowls, on top of bed of cauliflower rice, and garnish with fresh chopped parsley. Serve warm!

Nutritional Information per serving:

Calories: 208   Fat: 15g   Fiber: 1g   Carbs: 8g   Protein: 10g

122. Chicken Delight

Cook Time: 37 minutes
Servings: 4
Ingredients:

- 6 chicken thighs
- 2 tablespoons coconut oil
- ½ teaspoon thyme, dried
- 1 cup baby carrots
- 1 celery stalk, chopped
- 1 yellow onion, chopped

- Sea salt and black pepper to taste
- 2 tablespoons tomato paste
- 1 ½ lbs. potatoes, chopped
- 2 cups chicken stock
- 15-ounce can of tomatoes, diced
- ½ cup white wine

Directions:

Set your instant pot to the sauté mode, add the oil and heat it up. Add the chicken pieces, salt and pepper to taste, brown the chicken for 4-minutes on each side, then transfer chicken to a bowl. Add the thyme, onion, celery, carrots, tomato paste to your instant pot and stir. Cook for 5-minutes. Add the wine, and cook for an additional 3-minutes, stir. Add the chicken stock, chopped tomatoes, chicken pieces and stir. Place the steamer basket in the instant pot, add the potatoes to it. Cover the instant pot and cook on the Poultry setting for 30-minutes. Release the pressure naturally for 15-minutes. Take the potatoes out of the instant pot. Shred the chicken, add it to bowl with potatoes. Divide among serving plates. Serve warm!

Nutritional Information per serving:

Calories: 237   Fat: 12g   Fiber: 0g   Carbs: 1g   Protein: 30g

---

123. Party Chicken Wings

Cooking Time: 25 minutes
Servings: 6
Ingredients:

- 12 chicken wings, cut into 24 pieces
- 1lb. celery, cut into thin matchsticks
- 1 tablespoon parsley, fresh, diced
- 1 cup yogurt
- ¼ cup tomato puree
- 1 cup water
- Sea salt and black pepper to taste
- 4 tablespoons hot sauce
- ¼ cup honey

Directions:

Add water to the instant pot. Place the chicken wings in the steamer basket of the instant pot, cover and cook on Poultry setting for 19-minutes. In a mixing bowl add honey, hot sauce, tomato puree, salt and stir well. Release the pressure naturally for 10-minutes on your instant pot. Add the chicken wings to the honey mix and toss to coat them. Add the chicken wings to a lined baking sheet and place under a preheated broiler for 5-minutes. Arrange the celery sticks on a serving platter and add the chicken wings next to it. In a bowl, mix the parsley, with yogurt, stir and place on serving platter. Serve warm!

Nutritional Information per serving:

Calories: 300   Fat: 1 3.1g   Fiber: 2g   Carbs: 1.4g   Protein: 33g

---

124. Roasted Chicken

Cook Time: 35 minutes
Servings: 8
Ingredients:

- 1 whole chicken
- 2 teaspoons garlic powder
- 1 tablespoon coriander
- 1 tablespoon cumin
- Sea salt and black pepper to taste
- ½ teaspoon cinnamon, ground
- 1 tablespoon thyme, fresh
- 1 cup chicken stock
- 1 ½ tablespoons lemon zest
- 2 tablespoons extra virgin olive oil, divided

Directions:

In a mixing bowl, add the cinnamon, cumin, garlic, salt, pepper, coriander, and lemon zest, stir well. Rub the chicken with 1 tablespoon of oil, then rub it inside and out with the spice mix. Set your instant pot to the sauté mode, add the rest of the oil to it and heat it up. Add the chicken to the instant pot and brown it on all sides for 5-minutes. Add the thyme and stock, stir, cover and cook on the Poultry setting for 25-minutes. Release the pressure naturally for 10-minutes. Transfer chicken to a platter. Pour cooking liquid over it from instant pot. Serve warm!

Nutritional Information per serving:

Calories: 260   Fat: 13.1g   Fiber: 1g   Carbs: 4g   Protein: 26.7g

---

125. Braised Turkey Wings

Cook Time: 20 minutes   **Servings: 4**

Ingredients:

- 4 turkey wings
- 2 tablespoons butter
- 2 tablespoons olive oil
- 1 ½ cups cranberries, fresh
- 1 cup orange juice
- 1 cup walnuts
- 1 yellow onion, sliced
- Sea salt and black pepper to taste
- 1 bunch of thyme, chopped

Directions:

Set your instant pot onto the sauté mode, add the oil and butter and heat up. Add the turkey wings, salt, pepper and brown them on all sides for about 5-minutes. Remove the wings from instant pot, add the walnuts, onions, cranberries, thyme to instant pot and stir and cook for 2-minutes. Add the orange juice and return the wings to the instant pot, stir and cover. Cook on the Poultry setting for 20 minutes. Release the pressure naturally for 10-minutes. Divide the wings among serving plates. Heat the cranberry mixture in instant pot with Manual setting on low for 5-minutes. Drizzle the sauce over wings. Serve warm!

Nutritional Information per serving:

Calories: 320   Fat: 15.3g   Fiber: 2.1g   Carbs: 6.4g   Protein: 29g

---

126. Braised Quail

Cook Time: 15 minutes   **Servings: 2**

Ingredients:

- 2 quails, cleaned
- 2 cups water
- 3.5 ounces smoked pancetta, chopped
- ½ fennel bulb, cut into matchsticks
- 1 bunch rosemary
- Sea salt and black pepper to taste
- 1 bay leaf
- 1 bunch thyme
- 2 shallots, peeled and chopped
- ½ cup champagne
- 4 carrots, cut into thin matchsticks
- Juice of 1 lemon
- Olive oil
- ½ cup arugula
- 2 tablespoons olive oil

Directions:

Place the carrot and fennel into the instant pot steamer basket. Add water to the instant pot, cover and cook on the Steam setting for 1-minute, release the pressure using quick-release, rinse vegetables with cold water and transfer to a bowl. Put the cooking liquid in a separate bowl. Chop half the rosemary and thyme, then set aside. Set your instant pot to the sauté mode, add the oil and heat. Add the pancetta, shallots, thyme, rosemary, bay leaf, salt, pepper, and cook for 4-minutes.

Stuff the quail with the remaining whole rosemary and thyme and add to the instant pot. Brown all sides of the quail for 5-minutes. Add the champagne, stir and cook for an additional 2-minutes. Add the cooking liquid from the vegetables, cover and cook on the Poultry setting for 9-minutes. Release the pressure naturally for 15-minutes. Remove the quail from your instant pot. Set the instant pot to sauté mode and cook the sauce for 5-minutes stirring often. Arrange the arugula on a platter, add the steamed fennel, and carrots, a drizzle of oil, lemon juice on top with quail. Drizzle the sauce from instant pot over the quail. Serve warm!

Nutritional Information per serving:
Calories: 300   Fat: 17g   Fiber: 0.2g   Carbs: 0.2g   Protein: 40g

---

127. Crispy Chicken
Cook Time: 40 minutes
Servings: 4
Ingredients:

- 6 chicken thighs
- 4 garlic cloves, peeled, chopped
- 1 yellow onion, sliced thin
- 2 tablespoons cornstarch, mixed with 2 ½ tablespoons of water
- Sea salt and black pepper to taste
- 1 tablespoon soy sauce
- 1 cup cold water
- Dried rosemary
- 2 eggs, whisked
- 1 cup coconut flour
- 2 tablespoons butter
- 2 tablespoons coconut oil
- 1 ½ cups panko breadcrumbs

Directions:
In your instant pot mix the onion, garlic, rosemary and water. Place the chicken thighs into the steamer basket and place in the instant pot. Cover and cook on the Poultry setting for 9-minutes. Release the pressure naturally for 10-minutes. In a pan heat the oil and butter over medium-high heat. Add the breadcrumbs, stir and toast them, then remove them from the heat. Remove the chicken from instant pot; pat chicken thighs dry, season with salt and pepper, coat them with the flour, dip them in the whisked egg, then coat them in the toasted breadcrumbs.

Place chicken thighs on a lined baking sheet, bake in oven at 300° Fahrenheit for 10 minutes. Set your instant pot to the sauté mode, and heat up the cooking liquid. Add the salt, pepper, soy sauce, cornstarch and stir, then transfer to a bowl. Take the chicken thighs out of the oven, divide between serving plates. Serve with sauce from your instant pot. Serve warm!

Nutritional Information per serving:
Calories: 360   Fat: 7g   Fiber: 4g   Carbs: 1.8g   Protein: 15g

128. Chicken Salad

Cook Time: 25 minutes   **Servings: 2**

Ingredients:

- 1 chicken breast, skinless and boneless
- 3 cups water
- 3 tablespoons extra virgin olive oil
- 1 tablespoon honey
- 1 tablespoon balsamic vinegar
- 3 garlic cloves, minced
- Sea salt and black pepper to taste
- 1 tablespoon mustard
- Mixed salad greens
- Half a cup of cherry tomatoes, cut into halves

Directions:

In a bowl, mix 2 cups water with a pinch of salt. Add the chicken to the mixture, stir and place in the fridge for an hour. Add the remaining water to your instant pot, place the chicken breast in the steamer basket of your instant pot, cover and cook on the Poultry setting for 5-m inutes. Release the pressure naturally for 10-minutes. Remove the chicken breast from instant pot. Cut the chicken breast into thin strips. In a bowl mix salt, pepper, mustard, honey, vinegar, olive oil, garlic and whisk well. In a salad bowl, mix chicken strips with salad greens and tomatoes. Drizzle the vinaigrette on top. Serve room temperature.

Nutritional Information per serving:

Calories: 140   Fat: 7.5g   Fiber: 4g   Carbs: 1.1g   Protein: 19g

129. Stuffed Chicken Breasts

Cook Time: 30 minutes   **Servings: 2**

Ingredients:

- 2 chicken breasts, skinless, boneless, and butterflied
- 2 cups water
- 1-piece ham, cut in half, cooked
- Sea salt and black pepper to taste
- 16 bacon strips
- 4 mozzarella cheese slices
- 6 pieces of asparagus, cooked

Directions:

In a mixing bowl, mix the chicken with 1 cup water, salt, stir, cover and keep in the fridge for an hour. Pat the chicken breasts dry and place them on a working surface. Add 2 slices of mozzarella, 3 asparagus pieces onto each, 1 piece of ham, add salt and pepper then roll up each chicken breast. Place the bacon strips on a working surface, add the chicken and wrap them in bacon strips. Put the rolls in the steamer basket of your instant pot, add 1 cup of water to your instant pot, cover and cook on the Poultry setting for 10-minutes. Release the pressure naturally for 10-minutes. Pat rolls with paper towel and lay them on a plate. Set your instant pot to the sauté mode, add the chicken rolls to the instant pot and brown them for 5-minutes. Divide among serving plates. Serve warm!

Nutritional Information per serving:

Calories: 270   Fat: 11g   Fiber: 1g   Carbs: 6g   Protein: 37g

130. Turkey Mix and Mashed Potatoes

Cooking Time: 50 minutes   **Servings: 3**

Ingredients:

- 2 turkey quarters
- 1 cup chicken stock
- 1 celery stalk, chopped
- 3-garlic cloves, minced
- 1 carrot, chopped
- 1 yellow onion, chopped
- ½ cup white wine
- 2 tablespoons butter
- 3.5-ounces heavy cream
- 2 tablespoons Parmesan cheese, grated
- 5 Yukon gold potatoes, cut in halves
- 2 tablespoons cornstarch, mixed with 2 tablespoons water
- 1 teaspoon thyme, dried
- 1 teaspoon sage, dried
- 2 bay leaves
- 1 teaspoon rosemary, dried
- 2 tablespoons extra virgin olive oil
- Sea salt and black pepper to taste

Directions:

Season your turkey with salt and pepper. Add a tablespoon of oil to your instant pot. Set your instant pot to the sautè mode, and heat it up. Add the turkey and brown for 4-minutes, transfer turkey to a plate and set aside.

Add ½ a cup of chicken stock to your instant pot and stir. Add 1 tablespoon of oil, garlic, and cook for 2-minutes. Add the carrots, celery, pepper, salt and stir for 7-minutes. Add the sage, thyme, bay leaves and rosemary, stir. Add the wine and turkey back into the instant pot and the rest of the stock. Place the potatoes in the steamer basket for instant pot and place in the instant pot. Cook for 20 minutes on the Steam mode. Release the pressure naturally for 10-minutes. Transfer the potatoes to a bowl and mash them. Add some salt, butter, Parmesan cheese and cream, stir well. Divide the turkey quarters onto serving plates. Set your instant pot onto the sautè mode. Add the cornstarch mixture to pot, stir well, and cook for 3-minutes. Drizzle the sauce over the turkey and serve with mashed potatoes. Serve warm!

Nutritional Information per serving:

Calories: 200   Fat: 5g   Fiber: 4g   Carbs: 1.9g   Protein: 18g

131. Duck & Vegetables

Cooking Time: 40 minutes   **Serving: 8**

Ingredients:

- 1 duck, chopped into eight pieces
- 1-inch ginger piece, peeled chopped
- Salt and black pepper to taste
- 2 cups water
- 2 carrots, chopped
- 1 cucumber, chopped
- 1 tablespoon white wine

Directions:

In your instant pot place the pieces of duck. Add the carrots, wine, cucumber, ginger, water, salt, pepper, stir and cover, cook on Poultry mode for 40-minutes. Release the pressure naturally for 15-minutes. Divide the mix onto serving plates. Serve warm!

Nutritional Information per serving:

Calories: 189   Fat: 12g   Fiber: 1g   Carbs: 4g   Protein: 22g

132. Braised Duck and Potatoes

Cook Time: 20 minutes   **Servings: 4**

Ingredients:

- 2 duck breasts, boneless, skinless, cut into small chunks
- 1 tablespoon Truvia
- 4 garlic cloves, minced
- 1-inch ginger root, sliced
- 1 potato, cut into cubes
- Sea salt and black pepper to taste
- 4 tablespoons soy sauce
- ¼ cup water
- 4 tablespoons sherry wine
- 2 green onions, roughly chopped
- 1 tablespoon olive oil

Directions:

Set your instant pot to the sauté mode, add the oil and heat it up. Add the duck, stir and brown it for 5-minutes. Add the garlic, green onions, ginger, Truvia, water, wine, soy sauce, salt and pepper. Cover instant pot and set to the Poultry mode, and cook for 18-minutes. Release the pressure naturally for 10-minutes. Add the potatoes, stir, cover, and cook on the Steam setting for 5-minutes. Release the pressure using quick-release. Divide the duck amongst serving plates. Serve warm!

Nutritional Information per serving:

Calories: 238   Fat: 18g   Fiber: 0g   Carbs: 1g   Protein: 19g

133. Chicken in Tomatillo Sauce

Cook Time: 15 minutes   **Servings: 6**

Ingredients:

- 1lb. chicken thighs, skinless, boneless
- ½ cup cilantro, diced
- 4-ounces canned green chilies, chopped
- 1 garlic clove, peeled, crushed
- 1 yellow onion, sliced thinly
- 2 tablespoons coconut oil
- 4-ounces black olives, pitted, chopped
- 15-ounces cheddar cheese, grated
- 5-ounces tomatoes, cored, chopped
- 15-ounces cauliflower rice, already cooked
- 5-ounces canned garbanzo beans, drained
- 15-ounces canned tomatillos, chopped
- Sea salt and black pepper to taste

Directions:

Set your instant pot to the sauté mode, add the oil and heat it up. Add the onions, stir and cook for 5-minutes. Add the garlic and stir and cook for 1-minute. Add the chicken, chilies, cilantro, tomatillos, salt, pepper, and stir. Cover your instant pot and cook on the Poultry mode for 8-minutes. Release the pressure naturally for 10-minutes. Remove the chicken from your instant pot. On a cutting board shred the chicken. Return chicken to your instant pot then place the rice and beans on top. Set your instant pot to the sauté mode for 1-minute. Add the tomatoes, cheese, and olives to your instant pot, stir and cook for an additional 2-minutes. Divide among the serving plates. Serve warm!

Nutritional Information per serving:

Calories: 245   Fat: 31.4g   Fiber: 1.3g   Carbs: 14.2g   Protein: 20g

134. *Filipino Chicken*
Cooking Time: *15 minutes*
Servings: *4*
Ingredients:

- 5 lbs. chicken thighs
- ½ cup soy sauce
- 3 bay leaves
- 4 garlic cloves, minced
- 1 teaspoon black peppercorns, crushed
- ½ cup white vinegar
- Sea salt and black pepper to taste

Directions:
Set your instant pot on the Poultry mode, add the chicken, soy sauce, vinegar, garlic, peppercorns, salt, pepper, bay leaves, and stir. Cover the pot with lid an cook for 15-minutes. Release the pressure naturally for 10-minutes. Discard the bay leaves, stir, divide the chicken between serving plates. Serve hot!

Nutritional Information per serving:
Calories: 430   Fat: 19.2g   Fiber: 1g   Carbs: 2.4g   Protein: 76g

135. *Instant Pot Keto Chicken Stew*
Cook Time: *40 minutes*
Servings: *6*
Ingredients:

- 6 chicken thighs
- 2 ½ cups chicken stock
- 15-ounce can of tomatoes, chopped
- ½ teaspoon thyme, dried
- 1 celery stalk, chopped
- 2 tablespoons tomato paste
- 1 yellow onion, chopped
- Sea salt and black pepper to taste
- ¼ cup baby carrots
- 2 tablespoons coconut oil

Directions:
Set your instant pot to the sauté mode, add the coconut oil, and heat it. Add the chicken and brown on all sides for 4-minutes each, along with salt and pepper, then transfer the chicken to a plate. Add the tomato paste, onion, celery, thyme, carrots, salt, pepper, and sauté for 4-minutes and stir. Add the stock, chicken, tomatoes into instant pot, cover, and set to Manual setting on high for 25 minutes. Once the cooked time is complete, release the pressure for 15-minutes naturally. Transfer the chicken to a cutting board and allow it to cool down, then shred it using 2 forks, remove skin, bones and discard. Return the chicken to the instant pot and heat for an additional 3-minutes on high. Divide into serving bowls. Serve hot!

Nutritional Information per serving:
Calories: 212   Fat: 16g   Fiber: 2g   Carbs: 9g   Protein: 23g

136. Chicken Romano
Cook Time: 15 minutes
Servings: 4
Ingredients:

- 6 chicken thighs, skinless, boneless, cut into chunks
- ½ cup coconut flour
- 2 tablespoons vegetable oil
- 4-ounces mushrooms, sliced
- 1 cup Romano cheese, grated
- 1 yellow onion, chopped
- 1 teaspoon chicken bouillon granules
- 1 teaspoon basil, dried
- 1 teaspoon garlic, minced
- 1 tablespoon oregano, dried
- 1 teaspoon Truvia
- 1 teaspoon white wine vinegar
- 10-ounces tomato sauce

Directions:
Set your instant pot to the sauté mode, add the oil and heat. Add the chicken pieces, stir and brown on all sides for 5-minutes. Add the onion, garlic and stir, cooking for an additional 3-minutes. Add flour, pepper, salt and stir. Add the tomato sauce, vinegar, Truvia, basil, oregano, bouillon granules, mushrooms, and cover. Cook on the Poultry setting for 10-minutes. Release the pressure naturally, for 10-minutes. Add the cheese, stir, then divide among serving plates. Serve warm!

Nutritional Information per serving:
Calories: 450   Fat: 11g   Fiber: 1g   Carbs: 4.2g   Protein: 61.2g

---

137. Turkey Chili
Cook Time: 10 minutes
Servings: 4
Ingredients:

- 1lb. turkey meat, ground
- 2 ½ tablespoons chili powder
- 12-ounces vegetable stock
- Cayenne pepper
- 1 ½ teaspoons cumin
- 3 garlic cloves, chopped
- 1 yellow onion, chopped
- 15-ounces chickpeas, already cooked
- ½ cup of water
- Salt and black pepper to taste

Directions:
Place the turkey meat into your instant pot, add the water, stir and cover. Cook on the Poultry setting for 5-minutes. Release the pressure naturally for 10-minutes. Add the garlic, chickpeas, bell pepper, onion, chili powder, cayenne pepper, salt, pepper, and stock. Stir, and cover the instant pot, and cook in the Bean/Chili setting for 5-minutes. Release the pressure naturally for 10-minutes. Divide among serving bowls. Serve hot!

Nutritional Information per serving:
Calories: 22.4   Fat: 7g   Fiber: 6.1g   Carbs: 1.8g   Protein: 19.7g

138. Sweet & Tangy Chicken
Cook Time: *10 minutes*
Servings: *4*
Ingredients:

- 2 lbs. chicken thighs, boneless, skinless
- 2 teaspoons cilantro, diced
- 1 teaspoon mint, fresh, chopped
- 1 teaspoon ginger, grated
- ¼ cup extra virgin olive oil
- 2 tablespoons coconut nectar
- 1 cup lime juice
- ½ cup fish sauce

Directions:
Place the chicken thighs into your instant pot. In a mixing bowl mix the olive oil, lime juice, fish sauce, coconut nectar, mint, ginger, cilantro, and whisk well. Pour mixture over chicken, cover your instant pot, and cook on the Poultry setting for 10-minutes. Release the pressure naturally for 10-minutes. Divide among serving plates. Serve warm!

Nutritional Information per serving:
Calories: 300   Fat: 5g   Fiber: 4g   Carbs: 2.3g   Protein: 32g

---

139. Honey Barbecue Chicken Wings
Cooking Time: *25 minutes*
Servings: *4*
Ingredients:

- 2 lbs. chicken wings
- ½ cup water
- 2 teaspoons paprika
- 1 teaspoon red pepper flakes
- ½ cup apple juice
- Cayenne pepper
- ¾ cup honey barbecue sauce
- Sea salt and black pepper to taste
- 1 teaspoon Truvia
- ½ teaspoon basil, dried

Directions:
Place the chicken wings into your instant pot. Add the barbecue sauce, salt, pepper, paprika, red pepper, Truvia, water, and apple juice. Stir, cover and cook on the Poultry setting for 10-minutes. Release the pressure naturally for 10-minutes. Transfer the chicken wings to a baking sheet, add the sauce, place under preheated broiler for 7-minutes. Turn chicken wings over and broil for an additional 7-minutes. Divide among serving plates. Serve hot!

Nutritional Information per serving:
Calories: 147   Fat: 12.2g   Fiber: 1g   Carbs: 8g   Protein: 21.8g

140. Sticky Chicken Drumsticks

Cook Time: 20 minutes
Servings: 4
Ingredients:

- 8 chicken drumsticks
- 1 teaspoon ginger, fresh, grated
- 3 garlic cloves, finely chopped
- 3 tablespoons olive oil
- Juice of 1 lemon
- 2 tablespoons soy sauce

Directions:

Mix the lemon juice, olive oil, ginger, garlic, and soy sauce in your instant pot. Add the chicken drumsticks and stir to coat them. Secure the instant pot lid and set it to the Poultry setting for a cook time of 20-minutes. Release the pressure naturally for 15-minutes. Divide drumsticks on to serving plates, and drizzle sauce over them. Serve hot!

Nutritional Information per serving:

Calories: 132   Fat: 23g   Fiber: 1g   Carbs: 10g   Protein: 19g

---

141. Chicken, Broccoli, & Cheese

Cook Time: 45 minutes
Servings: 6
Ingredients:

- 20-ounces chicken breast, cooked, shredded
- 1 teaspoon oregano, dried
- ½ teaspoon paprika
- 1-ounce pork rinds
- 1 cup cheddar cheese, shredded
- ½ cup heavy cream
- ½ cup sour cream
- 2 cups broccoli, florets
- 2 tablespoons olive oil

Directions:

Place the cooked, shredded chicken into your instant pot. In a bowl mix broccoli, olive oil, and sour cream. Pour over chicken and stir. Pour heavy cream over top and season. On Manual setting cook on low for 40-minutes. Release the pressure naturally for 15-minutes. Crush the pork rinds. Add the pork rinds and cheese on top of mixture, cover with lid and cook for an additional 5-minutes. Divide among serving dishes. Serve warm!

Nutritional Information per serving:

Calories: 210   Fat: 33g   Fiber: 1g   Carbs: 7.3g   Protein: 32g

142. Instant Pot Cream Chicken & Sausage
Cook Time: 48 minutes
Servings: 4
Ingredients:

- 1 ½ lbs. chicken breasts, boneless, skinless, cut into strips
- 1 large Italian sausage, sliced
- 1-8 ounce package of cream cheese
- 2 tablespoons grainy mustard
- 1 small yellow onion, diced
- ½ cup white wine
- 1 cup chicken stock
- Scallions, chopped for garnish
- Salt and black pepper to taste
- 2 tablespoons coconut oil

Directions:
Set your instant pot to the sauté mode, add the oil and heat. Add the sausage, and chicken breast strips, and brown for about 5-minutes. Add the yellow onion, and cook for an additional 3-minutes and stir. In a mixing bowl combine the cheese, mustard, stock, wine, garlic, salt and pepper. Pour the cheese mix over the chicken and sausage mix, and stir to combine. Place the lid onto your instant pot and set it on Poultry setting for 40-minutes. Release the pressure naturally for 10-minutes. Stir mix and serve over a bed of cauliflower rice or zucchini pasta. Serve warm!

Nutritional Information per serving:
Calories: 232 Fat: 14g Fiber: 4g Carbs: 9g Protein: 12g

143. Instant Pot Chicken Hash
Cook Time: 43 minutes
Servings: 4
Ingredients:

- 1 lb. chicken, boneless, skinless, diced
- 2 cups chicken stock
- 1 cup sweet potatoes, peeled, diced
- 4 tablespoons of butter
- 1 cup yellow onion, chopped
- 1 cup red bell pepper, chopped
- Fresh parsley, chopped for garnish

Directions:
Set your instant pot to the sauté mode, add the butter and heat it. Add the chicken and stir, cooking for 5-minutes browning all sides of the chicken. Add the bell pepper, and onion, continue to cook for an additional 3-minutes, stir. Add the chicken stock and sweet potatoes, set the instant pot to the Meat/Stew setting for 35-minutes. Release the pressure naturally for 10-minutes, once the cooking is completed. Divide into serving dishes, and garnish with parsley. Serve warm!

Nutritional Information per serving:
Calories: 212 Fat: 37g Fiber: 8g Carbs: 12g Protein: 12g

144. Instant Pot Chicken Bean Chili
Cook Time: 35 minutes
Servings: 6
Ingredients:

- 1 lb. chicken, boneless, skinless, cubed
- 1 medium, yellow onion, diced
- 2 cups vegetable stock
- 1 15-ounce can of black beans, rinsed, drained
- 2 cups salsa
- 2 tablespoons olive oil

Directions:
Set your instant pot to the sauté mode, add the oil and heat it. Add the cubed chicken to instant pot, and brown on all sides for 5-minutes, stir often. Add the remaining ingredients to instant pot and stir. Close the lid place instant pot on the Bean/Chili setting for 30-minutes. Release the pressure naturally for 15-minutes. Divide among serving bowls. Serve hot!

Nutritional Information per serving:
Calories: 246   Fat: 26g   Fiber: 8g   Carbs: 12g   Protein: 28g

145. Instant Pot Herbal Chicken
Cook Time: 40 minutes
Servings: 4
Ingredients:

- 1 lb. chicken, cubed
- 2 cups chicken stock
- 3 tablespoons rosemary leaves, fresh, chopped
- 3 tablespoons thyme leaves, fresh, chopped
- 3 garlic cloves, minced
- Salt and black pepper to taste
- 1 red bell pepper, chopped
- 1 green bell pepper, chopped
- 1 cup broccoli, florets

Directions:
Blend the garlic and herbs, and rub the mixture over your chicken chunks. In your instant pot heat olive oil with the sauté mode setting. Add the chicken into instant pot, stir and cook for 5-minutes, browning chicken on all sides. Add the chicken stock and veggies, and close the lid on your instant pot. Set to Poultry setting for 35-minutes. Release the pressure naturally for 10-minutes. Divide into serving dishes. Serve warm!

Nutritional Information per serving:
Calories: 217   Fat: 18g   Fiber: 2g   Carbs: 6g   Protein: 9g

146. Instant Pot Chicken Fillets
Cook Time: 45 minutes
Servings: 4
Ingredients:
- 1 lb. chicken fillets, cut into four equal portions
- ¼ cup sour cream, reduced fat
- 2 teaspoons lemon juice
- 2 tablespoons stone-ground mustard
- Salt and pepper to taste
- Lime wedges for garnish

Directions:
Place the chicken fillets into your instant pot. Make a paste with the remaining ingredients except the lime wedges. Spread the mixture over the chicken fillets. Set the instant pot to the Poultry setting for 45-minutes. Release the pressure naturally for 10-minutes. Divide among serving plates, and garnish with lemon wedges.

Nutritional Information per serving:
Calories: 253   Fat: 27g   Fiber: 6g   Carbs: 11g   Protein: 22g

147. Buttery Chicken with Macadamia
Cook Time: 22 minutes
Servings: 4
Ingredients:
- 1lb. chicken breast, sliced into four equal portions
- 2 tablespoons macadamia nuts, toasted
- ¼ teaspoon chili powder
- 2 tablespoons lime juice + ½ teaspoon lime zest
- 2 tablespoons butter

Directions:
Set your instant pot to the sauté setting, add the butter and heat it. Season the chicken with salt and black pepper. Add the chicken to instant pot and cook for 5-minutes or until the chicken is slightly brown in color on all sides. Set on the Poultry setting on low for 17-minutes. Release the pressure naturally for 10-minutes. Make a mixture using the melted butter from instant pot, lime juice, chili powder, lime zest and pour over the chicken on serving plates. Add the toasted macadamia nuts as garnish. Serve warm!

Nutritional Information per serving:
Calories: 254   Fat: 23g   Fiber: 2g   Carbs: 10g   Protein: 19g

148. Mushroom & Chicken Hash
Cook Time: *40 minutes*
Servings: *4*
Ingredients:
- 2 cups cooked chicken, cubed
- 4 tablespoons butter
- 4 celery ribs, finely chopped
- 1 medium yellow onion, diced
- 1 lb. button mushrooms, sliced

Directions:
Set your instant pot to the sauté mode, add the butter and heat. Add the mushrooms and sauté for 2-minutes. Add the onion, chicken, and celery, stir and cook for an additional 3-minutes. Close the lid and set instant pot on the Poultry setting for 35-minutes. Release the pressure for 10-minutes. Divide into serving plates. Serve warm!

Nutritional Information per serving:
Calories: 232   Fat: 9g   Fiber: 1g   Carbs: 2g   Protein: 21g

---

149. Cheesy Spinach Stuffed Chicken Breasts
Cook Time: *20 minutes*
Servings: *2*
Ingredients:
- 2 chicken breasts
- 1 teaspoon onion powder
- 1 teaspoon garlic powder
- 2 cups baby spinach
- 3 tablespoons coconut oil
- 1 cup parmesan cheese, shredded
- 1 cup mozzarella cheese, shredded
- 1 red bell pepper, chopped
- 2 cups water
- Sea salt and black pepper to taste

Directions:
Cover your instant pot trivet with foil. Set your instant pot to the sauté mode, add 2 tablespoons of the coconut oil and heat it. Add the chicken and brown on all sides for 5-minutes. Remove the chicken, and allow to cool. Press the Keep Warm/Cancel button to end the sauté mode. In a mixing bowl, combine parmesan cheese, red pepper, mozzarella cheese, remaining 1 tablespoon of coconut oil, baby spinach and seasoning. When the chicken is cool, cut down the middle, but do not cut all the way through. Stuff with spinach mixture. Pour 2 cups of water in the instant pot. Place the trivet inside. Place the chicken on trivet. Close and seal lid. Press the Manual setting, and cook on high pressure for 7-minutes. Release the pressure naturally for 10-minutes. Allow the chicken to rest for 5-minutes. Divide among serving plates. Serve warm!

Nutritional Information per serving:
Calories: 500   Fat: 33g   Fiber: 1.7g   Carbs: 3.8g   Protein: 45g

Chapter 7. Seafood Instant Pot Recipes

150. Spicy Lemon Salmon
***Cook Time:* 10 minutes**
***Servings:* 4**
Ingredients:

- 4 salmon fillets
- 1 teaspoon cayenne pepper
- 1 tablespoon paprika
- 1 cup water
- Juice from 2 lemons
- Sea salt and black pepper to taste

Directions:
Rinse your salmon, and pat dry. In a mixing bowl, combine cayenne pepper, paprika, salt and pepper. Drizzle the lemon juice over the salmon fillets. Turn over fillets, repeat on the other side. Add 1 cup of water to your instant pot. Place the trivet inside your instant pot. Place your salmon fillets on top of the trivet. Close and seal instant pot, press the Manual button. Cook at high-pressure for 10-minutes. Once cooking time is complete use the quick-release for pressure. Divide up among serving plates. Serve warm!

Nutritional Information per serving:
Calories: 280   Fat: 20g   Fiber: 0.5g   Carbs: 8g   Protein: 20.5g

151. Coconut Shrimp Curry
***Cook Time:* 34 minutes**
***Servings:* 4**
Ingredients:

- 1 lb. of shrimp, peeled, deveined
- 10-ounces coconut milk
- 1 red bell pepper, sliced
- 4 tomatoes, chopped
- 1 teaspoon, fresh ground black pepper
- Juice from 1 lime
- 4 garlic cloves, minced
- 1 tablespoon coconut oil
- ½ cup cilantro, fresh, chopped for garnish

Directions:
Set your instant pot to the sauté mode, add the oil and heat it. Season your shrimp with lime juice, salt and pepper. Sauté the garlic for 1-minute. Add the shrimp and cook for 4-minutes per side. Add the bell peppers and tomatoes. Stir well. Press the Keep Warm/Cancel button to cancel the sauté mode. Add the coconut milk and stir. Close and seal the lid of instant pot. Press the Manual setting, and cook on high pressure for 25-minutes. Once cooking is completed, use the quick-release for pressure. Divide into serving plates, and garnish with fresh, chopped cilantro.

Nutritional Information per serving:
Calories: 150   Fat: 3g   Fiber: 3g   Carbs: 1g   Protein: 7g

152. Mediterranean Fish
Cook Time:
Servings: *4*
Ingredients:

- 4 fish fillets (any kind)
- 1 teaspoon parsley, fresh, chopped
- 1 tablespoon thyme, fresh, chopped
- 1 tablespoon coconut oil
- 1 cup water
- 2 garlic cloves, minced
- 1 cup green olives, pitted
- 1 lb. cherry tomatoes, halved
- Sea salt and black pepper to taste

Directions:
Pour 1 cup of water in your instant pot. Cover the instant pot trivet with foil. On a flat surface, rub fish fillets with garlic. Season with thyme, pepper and salt. Place the olives and cherry tomatoes along the bottom of Instant pot. Place the fillets on the trivet. Close the lid and seal. Set on Manual, and cook at high-pressure for 15-minutes. When done, release pressure naturally for 10-minutes. Place the fish with ingredients, stir to coat them. Place on serving plates, and top with fresh, chopped parsley for garnish. Serve warm!

Nutritional Information per serving:
Calories: 225   Fat: 4g   Fiber: 2g   Carbs: 9g   Protein: 30g

153. Ginger, Sesame Glaze Salmon
Cook Time: *25 minutes*
Servings: *4*
Ingredients:

- 4 salmon fillets
- 2 tablespoons soy sauce
- 1 tablespoon rice vinegar
- 2 tablespoons white wine
- 1 tablespoon sugar-free ketchup
- 1 tablespoon fish sauce
- 4 garlic cloves, minced
- 2 teaspoons sesame oil
- 2 cups water

Directions:
In a mixing bowl, combine fish sauce, garlic, ginger, ketchup, white wine, rice vinegar, soy sauce, and sesame oil. In a large Ziploc bag, add the sauce and salmon fillets. Marinate for 10-hours. Pour 2 cups water in to your instant pot. Cover the trivet with foil. Place the trivet into your instant pot. Place the marinated salmon on the trivet. Close the lid and seal. Press the Manual button, cook on high-pressure for 15-minutes. Once done release the pressure naturally for 10-minutes. Divide onto serving plates. Serve warm!

Nutritional Information per serving:
Calories: 370   Fat: 23.5g   Fiber: 0g   Carbs: 2.6g   Protein: 33g

154. Cauliflower Risotto and Salmon
Cook Time: 30 minutes   **Servings: 4**
Ingredients:

- 4 salmon fillets, shredded
- 1 lb. asparagus, stemmed, chopped
- ½ cup parmesan cheese, shredded
- 1 cup chicken broth
- 1 tablespoon coconut oil
- Sea salt and black pepper to taste
- 2 teaspoons thyme, fresh, chopped
- 1 tablespoon rosemary, fresh, chopped
- 8-ounces coconut cream, unsweetened
- 1 head of cauliflower, chopped into florets

Directions:

In a food processor add the cauliflower florets, and pulse until you have rice-like consistency. Set your instant pot to the sautė mode, add the oil and heat it. Add the cauliflower rice, asparagus, and shredded salmon fillet. Cook until light brown and tender. Press the Keep Warm/Cancel setting to stop the sautė mode. Add the remaining ingredients and stir well. Close and seal lid. Press the manual button, cook on high-pressure for 20-minutes. Once done, release the pressure naturally for 10-minutes. Stir, and divide into serving bowls. Serve warm!

Nutritional Information per serving:
Calories: 225   Fat: 16g   Fiber: 4g   Carbs: 9g   Protein: 6g

155. Chili, Lime Cod
Cook Time: 22 minutes   **Servings: 4**
Ingredients:

- 4 cod fillets, shredded
- ¼ cup parsley, fresh, chopped
- ½ cup low-carb mayonnaise
- 1 tablespoon rice wine vinegar
- 1 yellow onion, chopped
- 1 celery stalk, chopped
- 4 garlic cloves, minced
- 1 can (14-ounce) tomatoes, diced
- 1 teaspoon paprika
- 1 tablespoon coconut oil
- 1 cup vegetable stock
- Zest from 1 lime
- Sea salt and black pepper to taste

Directions:

Press the sautė mode on your instant pot, and heat the coconut oil. Add the onion, and garlic. Sautė for 2-minutes, and add the celery and shredded cod. Press the Keep Warm/Cancel button to stop the sautė mode. Add the diced tomatoes, rice wine, mayonnaise, parsley, lime juice and zest, along with seasoning. Stir well. Close the lid and seal. Press the Manual button and cook at high-pressure for 20-minutes. Release the pressure naturally for 10-minutes. Divide onto serving plates. Serve warm!

Nutritional Information per serving:
Calories: 215   Fat: 15g   Fiber: 2g   Carbs: 3g   Protein: 35g

156. Instant Pot Halibut Fillets
Cook Time: 30 minutes
Servings: 4
Ingredients:
- 4 halibut fillets
- 1 lemon sliced for garnish
- 2 cups of water
- Zest and juice of 1 lime
- ¼ cup mozzarella cheese, grated
- ¼ cup parmesan cheese, fresh, grated
- ¼ cup ghee, melted
- ¼ cup low-carb mayonnaise
- 4 green onions, chopped
- 6 garlic cloves, minced
- Sea salt and black pepper to taste

Directions:
Pour 2-cups of water in the instant pot. Cover the trivet with foil. In mixing bowl, combine green onions, garlic, ghee, mayonnaise, cheeses, lime juice, lime zest, salt and pepper. Stir well. Coat the halibut fillets with the mixture. Place halibut on trivet. Close and seal the lid. Press the Manual button, cook on high-pressure for 20-minutes. Use the quick-release for pressure. Divide up into serving plates, and garnish with fresh, chopped parsley. Serve warm!

Nutritional Information per serving:
Calories: 250   Fat: 12g   Fiber: 1g   Carbs: 5g   Protein: 25g

157. Fish Fillets & Orange Sauce
Cook Time: 10 minutes
Servings: 4
Ingredients:
- 4 spring onions, finely chopped
- Zest from 1 orange
- Juice from 1 orange
- 4 white fish fillets
- 1 tablespoon olive oil
- 1-inch ginger piece, grated
- Sea salt and black pepper to taste
- 1 cup fish stock

Directions:
Season the fish fillets with salt and pepper, then rub them with oil and place on a plate. Place the onions, orange zest, orange juice, fish stock into your instant pot. Add the steamer basket and place the fish fillets inside it. Cover the instant pot with lid and cook on high-pressure on Manual setting for 10-minutes. Release the pressure using the quick-release. Divide the fish fillets among serving plates, then drizzle the orange sauce from instant pot over fillets. Serve warm!

Nutritional Information per serving:
Calories: 343   Fat: 21g   Fiber: 1g   Carbs: 8g   Protein: 26g

158. Calamari & Tomatoes
Cook Time: 30 minutes
Servings: 4
Ingredients:

- 1 ½ lbs. of calamari, cleaned, heads detached, tentacles separated and cut into thin strips
- 1 tablespoon olive oil
- Juice of 1 lemon
- 2 anchovies, chopped
- A pinch of red pepper flakes
- 1 bunch parsley, chopped
- ½ cup white wine
- 1 garlic clove, minced
- Sea salt and black pepper to taste
- 1 (15-ounce can) tomatoes, chopped

Directions:
Set your instant pot to the sautė mode, add the oil and heat it up. Add the anchovies, garlic, and pepper flakes, stir and cook for 3-minutes. Add the calamari, stir and sautė for 5-minutes more. Add the wine, stir and cook for 3 minutes more. Add the tomatoes, half of the parsley, some salt and pepper, stir and cover pot. Set to manual on high-pressure for 20-minutes. Release the pressure naturally for 15-minutes. Add the lemon juice and zest, remaining parsley and stir. Divide up among serving plates. Serve warm!

Nutritional Information per serving:
Calories: 342   Fat: 18g   Fiber: 1g   Carbs: 3g   Protein: 28g

159. Red Snapper & Chili Sauce
Cook Time: 12 minutes
Servings: 2
Ingredients:

- 1 red snapper, cleaned
- 1 teaspoon Truvia
- 2 cups water
- 1 green onion, chopped
- 1 teaspoon sesame oil
- 2 teaspoons sesame seeds, toasted
- 2 teaspoons Korean plum extract
- ½ teaspoon ginger, grated
- 1 garlic clove, minced
- 1 tablespoon soy sauce
- 3 tablespoons Korean chili paste
- Dash of sea salt

Directions:
Make some slits into your red snapper, season with salt and leave aside for 30-minutes. Put the water into your instant pot, add the steamer basket inside and place the fish in it. Rub the fish with the chili paste, cover your instant pot with lid and secure and cook on Manual on low for 12-minutes. In a mixing bowl, combine Truvia, soy sauce, garlic, plum extract, sesame seeds, sesame oil, green onions, and stir well. Release pressure naturally for 10-minutes. Divide fish among serving plates, and drizzle with sauce you made. Serve warm!

Nutritional Information per serving:
Calories: 284   Fat: 17g   Fiber: 1g   Carbs: 9g   Protein: 27g

160. Baked Red Snapper
Cook Time: *12 minutes*
Servings: *4*
Ingredients:

- 4 red snappers, cleaned
- 5 garlic cloves, minced
- ½ cup parsley, chopped
- ½ cup olive oil
- 1 lemon, sliced
- 4 tablespoons lemon juice
- Sea salt and black pepper to taste
- 5-ounces of grape leaves, blanched

Directions:
Pat the fish dry and place it in a bowl. Season the fish with salt, pepper, and brush half the oil onto it and rub well, then keep in the fridge for 30-minutes. In a mixing bowl, combine parsley, salt and pepper, stir. Divide this mix into the fish cavities, wrap each in a grape leaf, drizzle with lemon juice over them and place the fish in a heat-proof dish within your instant pot steamer basket. Drizzle the rest of the oil over the fish, cover the dish with some tin foil, place the basket inside your instant pot. Add 2 cups of water to your instant pot, cover with lid, and cook on High-pressure for 12-minutes. Release the pressure using the quick-release. Divide the wrapped fish among serving plates, top with lemon slices. Serve warm!

Nutritional Information per serving:
Calories: 276 Fat: 20g Fiber: 1g Carbs: 8g Protein: 29g

161. Red Snapper & Tomato Sauce
Cook Time: *11 minutes*
Servings: *4*
Ingredients:

- 4 medium red snapper fillets
- 4 ciabatta rolls, cut in halves, and toasted
- 2 tablespoons parsley, fresh, chopped
- 16-ounces canned tomatoes, crushed
- ¼ cup olive oil
- 1 yellow onion, chopped
- 3 tablespoons hot water
- A pinch of saffron threads
- Sea salt and black pepper to taste

Directions:
In a mixing bowl, combine, hot water, and saffron, then leave aside. Set your instant pot to the sauté mode, and add the oil and heat it up. Add the onion, and stir and cook for 2-minutes. Add the fish, cook for an additional 2-minutes and flip on the other side and cook that side for 2-minutes. Add the tomatoes, drained saffron, some salt and pepper, cover the instant pot with lid. Set the instant pot to low for 5-minutes. Release the pressure with the quick-release. Divide the fish and sauce among serving plates, and garnish with fresh, chopped parsley, serve with ciabatta rolls. Serve warm!

Nutritional Information per serving:
Calories: 243 Fat: 14g Fiber: 2g Carbs: 7g Protein: 26g

162. Thai Red Snapper

Cook Time: 20 minutes   **Servings: 2**

Ingredients:

For the Marinade:
- 1 tablespoon Thai curry paste
- 1 cup coconut milk
- 1 tablespoon fish sauce paste
- 1 tablespoon cilantro, chopped
- 2 cups water
- 1 lime, sliced

For the Salsa:
- 2 jalapenos, chopped
- 2 mangoes, peeled, and chopped
- 1 scallion, chopped

- 2 red snapper fillets
- 1 teaspoon garlic, minced
- 1 tablespoon ginger, grated
- 1 teaspoon Truvia
- Juice of ½ a lime
- Zest of a lime

- A handful of cilantro, fresh, chopped for garnish
- Juice from 1 lime

Directions:

In a mixing bowl, combine fish sauce with coconut milk, zest from 1 lime, curry paste, juice from ½ a lime, Truvia, garlic, ginger, and whisk well. Add the fish fillets, toss to coat and set aside for 30-minutes. In another bowl, mix jalapenos, mangoes, scallion, juice from 1 lime, mix well and leave aside. Place the water in your instant pot and put the steamer basket inside. Place the fish in 2-pieces of parchment paper, cover them with lime slices and wrap them. Place them into the steamer basket, cover the instant pot with lid, and cook on high for 10-minutes. Release the pressure using the quick-release. Put the marinade from fish into a pan and heat it up over medium-high heat. Boil for a couple of minutes and take off heat. Drizzle some of the sauce over dish, top with mango salsa and garnish with fresh, chopped cilantro. Serve warm!

Nutritional Information per serving:

Calories: 257   Fat: 17g   Fiber: 1g   Carbs: 10g   Protein: 28g

---

163. Lobster & Sweet Potatoes

Cook Time: 16 minutes   **Servings: 4**

Ingredients:
- 4 lobsters
- 1 onion, cut into wedges
- Water
- 2 garlic heads, not peeled

- 1 ½ lbs of sweet potatoes, peeled, and cubed
- 4 ears of corn, shucked, and halved
- 4 tablespoons butter

Directions:

Place the cubed-sweet potatoes in your instant pot. Add onion, garlic, and some salt with enough water to cover them. Cover your pot and cook on high for 12-minutes. Release the pressure using quick-release. Add the lobsters, and corn to the instant pot and cover once again. Cook on high for 5-minutes. Release the pressure again using quick-release. Divide the corn and sweet potatoes among serving plates, season with some salt and drizzle some melted butter over them. Discard the onion, and garlic. Transfer the lobsters to cutting board and remove the meat. Divide lobster meat among serving plates next to corn and sweet potatoes. Drizzle the rest of butter over lobster meat. Serve warm!

Nutritional Information per serving:
Calories: 297   Fat: 18g   Fiber: 2g   Carbs: 11g   Protein: 32g

---

164. Steamed Lobster
Cooking Time: 3 minutes
Servings: 1
Ingredients:
- 1 cup non-alcoholic beer
- 2 cups water
- 1 lobster
- Sea salt and white pepper to taste

Directions:
Add the beer and water to your instant pot and place the steamer basket inside it as well. Place the lobster in the basket, cover and cook on high for 3-minutes. Release the pressure with quick-release. Transfer lobster to serving plate and season with some salt and pepper. Serve warm!

Nutritional Information per serving:
Calories: 286   Fat: 19g   Fiber: 1g   Carbs: 16g   Protein: 37g

---

165. Simple Instant Pot Lobster
Cook Time: 3 minutes
Servings: 3
Ingredients:
- 2 lbs. lobster tails
- ½ cup ghee, melted
- 1 cup water
- A dash of sea salt and some black pepper

Directions:
Put the water into your instant pot, add the lobster tails into steamer basket and place in your instant pot. Cook on high for 3-minutes. Release the pressure using the quick-release. Transfer the lobster tails to a bowl, drizzle melted ghee over lobster, and sprinkle with some salt and pepper. Serve warm!

Nutritional Information per serving:
Calories: 289   Fat: 14g   Fiber: 2g   Carbs: 8g   Protein: 30g

166. Spicy Sardines
Cook Time: 15 minutes
Servings: 4
Ingredients:

- 1 lb. of sardines
- 8 garlic cloves, minced
- 2 yellow onions, cut in halves, then thinly sliced
- 2 tablespoons white vinegar
- 3 tablespoons coconut oil
- ½ teaspoon turmeric
- 1 large tomato, chopped
- 1 ½ teaspoons chili powder
- 4 curry leaves
- 1 green chili pepper, chopped
- 1-inch ginger pieces, grated

Directions:
Place the oil into your instant pot, and heat it up on the sauté mode. Add the garlic, ginger, onion, curry leaves, chili, and stir for 2-minutes. Add the chili powder, tomato, turmeric, vinegar, salt, pepper, and stir and cook for an additional 3-minutes. Add the sardines, cover your instant pot and cook on high for 10-minutes. Release the pressure with quick-release. Divide among serving plates. Serve warm!
Nutritional Information per serving:
Calories: 206   Fat: 15g   Fiber: 2g   Carbs: 13g   Protein: 27g

167. Tasty Sardines
Cook Time: 20 minutes
Servings: 5
Ingredients:

- 2 lbs. sardines
- 2 peppercorns
- 10 garlic cloves, minced
- 1 tablespoon, smoked paprika
- 1 teaspoon Truvia
- 1 red chili pepper, chopped
- 2 bay leaves
- 1 pickle, sliced
- 1 carrot, chopped
- 2 cups tomato sauce
- 2 tablespoons olive oil
- 2 cups water

Directions:
Put sardines into a mixing bowl, cover them with water and salt to taste, leave them to sit for 15-minutes. Drain the sardines and put them into your instant pot. Add the peppercorns, cloves, oil, tomato sauce, carrots, bay leaves, chili pepper, pickle, Truvia, paprika, garlic, and stir gently. Cover with pot lid and cook on low for 20-minutes. Release the pressure naturally for 10-minutes. Divide among serving plates. Serve warm!
Nutritional Information per serving:
Calories: 284   Fat: 12g   Fiber: 1g   Carbs: 1.4g   Protein: 29g

168. Teriyaki Salmon
Cook Time: 10 minutes
Servings: 2
Ingredients:
- ¼ cup water
- 2 teaspoons sesame seeds
- 1 tablespoon sesame oil
- 1 garlic clove, minced
- ½ cup soy sauce
- 2 salmon fillets
- 1 tablespoon cornstarch mixed with 1 tablespoon of water
- 3 green onions, chopped
- 1 cup water for instant pot
- 1 teaspoon Truvia
- 1 tablespoon ginger, grated
- ¼ cup mirin

Directions:
In a mixing bowl, combine mirin, soy sauce, sesame oil, sesame seeds, ginger, garlic, Truvia, and ¼ cup water, stir well. Add the salmon and toss to coat, cover and keep the salmon in the fridge for 30-minutes. Add 1 cup water to your instant pot and place the steamer basket inside. Add a pan in the basket, put the salmon in the pan and reserve the marinade. Cover your instant pot with lid and cook on high for 8-minutes. Put the marinade in a pot and heat it over medium-high heat. Add the cornstarch to it, mix and stir. Release the pressure using quick-release. Divide the salmon among serving plates, and drizzle with the sauce on top. Serve warm!

Nutritional Information per serving:
Calories: 304   Fat: 21g   Fiber: 2g   Carbs: 1.6g   Protein: 46g

169. Simple Salmon & Onion
Cook Time: 6 minutes
Servings: 4
Ingredients:
- 4 salmon steaks
- ½ cup white wine
- 1 yellow onion, sliced thinly
- ½ cup water
- 1 lemon, sliced
- Sea salt and black pepper to taste

Directions:
Add the wine, water, and some salt and pepper into your instant pot. Stir, and place the steamer basket inside your instant pot. Put the salmon steaks in the basket, season with salt and pepper, cover them with onions, and lemon slices. Cover and cook on high for 6-minutes. Release the pressure using quick-release. Divide the salmon steaks among serving plates and top them with onions and lemon slices. Serve warm!

Nutritional Information per serving:
Calories: 321   Fat: 19g   Fiber: 1g   Carbs: 1.2g   Protein: 43g

170. Simple Instant Pot Salmon
Cook Time: 5 minutes
Servings: 2
Ingredients:

- 2 salmon fillets
- 1 tablespoon thyme, fresh, chopped
- 1 bay leaf
- 2 tablespoons mustard
- Sea salt and black pepper to taste
- 1 cup fish stock
- Slices of lemon for garnish

Directions:
In a mixing bowl, combine mustard, thyme, salt, pepper, and stir. Rub the salmon fillets with this mix. Put the stock and bay leaf into your instant pot. Place the steamer basket inside instant pot and place salmon in it. Cover and cook on high for 5 minutes. Release the pressure using quick-release. Divide the salmon among serving plates and garnish with sliced lemons. Serve warm!
Nutritional Information per serving:
Calories: 326   Fat: 20g   Fiber: 2g   Carbs: 1.4g   Protein: 47g

171. Salmon Fillets with Sauce
Cook Time: 6 minutes
Servings: 4
Ingredients:

- 4 salmon fillets
- 1 cup water
- 3 tablespoons mayonnaise
- 2 tablespoons butter
- 1 teaspoon Truvia
- 1 tablespoon dill, fresh, chopped
- 1 teaspoon soy sauce
- 1 tablespoon lemon juice

Directions:
Add the water to your instant pot, add the steamer basket inside and add the fish to basket. Cover and cook on high for 5-minutes. Add the lemon juice, butter, Truvia, dill, soy sauce, mayo to a pot, stir well and heat over medium-high heat. Release the pressure of the instant pot naturally for 10-minutes. Divide the salmon among the serving plates and drizzle over the top of fish the sauce. Serve warm!
Nutritional Information per serving:
Calories: 327   Fat: 16g   Fiber: 1g   Carbs: 1.6g   Protein: 43g

172. Tuna Steaks

Cook Time: 5 minutes
Servings: 4
Ingredients:

- 4 medium tuna steaks
- 1 bunch oregano, fresh
- 3 tablespoons lemon juice
- 2 tablespoons soy sauce
- 1/3 cup white wine
- Sea salt and black pepper to taste
- Some lettuce and tomatoes for serving

Directions:

Place your tuna steaks into your instant pot, add the soy sauce, wine, lemon juice, salt, pepper, and add the steamer basket as well, place the fresh oregano in the steamer basket. Cook on high for 5-minutes. Release the pressure using the quick-release. Divide the tuna steaks among the serving plates, serve with lettuce and tomatoes on the side. Serve warm!

Nutritional Information per serving:

Calories: 298   Fat: 12g   Fiber: 2g   Carbs: 1.0g   Protein: 26g

173. Tuna Casserole

Cook Time: 4 minutes
Servings: 4
Ingredients:

- 2 ½ cups macaroni pasta
- 10-ounces cream of mushroom soup
- 14-ounces of canned tuna, drained
- 1 cup cheddar cheese, shredded
- 1 cup peas
- 3 cups water
- Salt and black pepper to taste

Directions:

In your instant pot mix the water, mushroom soup, tuna, macaroni, peas, salt, pepper, and stir. Cover and cook on high for 4-minutes. Release the pressure using the quick-release. Add the shredded cheese then cover your pot and allow it to sit for 5-minutes. Divide among serving bowls. Serve warm or cold!

Nutritional Information per serving:

Calories: 287   Fat: 12g   Fiber: 2g   Carbs: 7g   Protein: 28g

174. *Zucchini Pasta with Capers*
Cooking Time: 8 minutes
Servings: 4
Ingredients:

- 2 tablespoons capers
- Water
- 16-ounces of zucchini pasta
- 11-ounces of canned tuna in oil
- 3 anchovies
- 1 tablespoon olive oil
- 1 garlic clove, minced
- 2 cups tomato puree
- Sea salt to taste

Directions:
Set your instant pot to the saute mode, add the oil and heat it up. Add the anchovies and garlic, stir and sauté them for 2-minutes. Add tomato puree, tuna, salt and stir. Add the water cover and cook for 3-minutes on low. Release the pressure on quick-release. Divide then place the tuna mix on top of bed of zucchini pasta and top with capers. Serve warm!

Nutritional Information per serving:
Calories: 267   Fat: 7g   Fiber: 1g   Carbs: 1.4g   Protein: 23g

---

175. *Beans & Clams*
Cook Time: 10 minutes
Servings: 6
Ingredients:

- 10-ounces canned white beans, drained
- 1 bay leaf
- 2 garlic cloves, minced
- 1 tablespoon olive oil
- 4-ounces white wine
- 14-ounces clams
- A dash of salt

Directions:
Place the beans in your instant pot, add water to cover, a pinch of salt and bay leaf, stir. Cover and cook on high for 10-minutes. Release the pressure using quick-release. Drain the beans and clean your pot. Add the oil and set to sauté mode, and heat oil up. Add the garlic, stir and cook for 2-minutes. Add wine, beans, clams, cover and cook on high for 6-minutes. Release the pressure again using quick-release. Divide the clams and beans in serving bowls. Serve warm!

Nutritional Information per serving:
Calories: 254   Fat: 26g   Fiber: 2g   Carbs: 8g   Protein: 21g

176. Instant Pot Squid

Cook Time: 25 minutes
Servings: 4
Ingredients:

- 1 small ginger piece, grated
- 2 yellow onions, chopped
- 1 lb. squid, cut into medium pieces
- 10-garlic cloves, minced
- 2 green chilies, chopped
- 3 tablespoons olive oil
- ¾ cup water
- 1 teaspoon mustard seeds
- 1 teaspoon garam masala
- Black pepper to taste
- A pinch of sea salt
- Pinch of turmeric powder
- ¾ tablespoon chili powder
- ½ tablespoon lemon juice
- ¼ cup coconut, shredded
- 1 tablespoon coriander, ground

Directions:
Place your instant pot on the sauté mode, add the oil and heat it up. Add the mustard seeds, stir and toast them for 1-minute. Add the coconut, stir, toast for 2-minutes more. Add the ginger, chilies, onions, garlic and stir and cook for 1-minute. Add the curry leaf, pepper, salt, lemon juice, coriander, chili powder, turmeric, garam masala, water, squid and stir. Cover and cook on low for 25-minutes. Release the pressure naturally for 10-minutes. Divide into serving bowls. Serve warm!

Nutritional Information per serving:
Calories: 241 Fat: 42g Fiber: 1g Carbs: 11g Protein: 30g

177. Italian Braised Squid

Cook Time: 20 minutes
Servings: 4
Ingredients:

- 1 lb. peas
- 1 lb. squid, cut into medium pieces
- 1 tablespoon olive oil
- 1 tablespoon white wine
- ½ lb. tomatoes, crushed
- Sea salt and pepper to taste
- 1 yellow onion, chopped

Directions:
Add the oil to your instant pot, set it on sauté mode, and heat the oil up. Add the onion, stir and cook for 3-minutes. Add the squid and cook for an additional 3-minutes. Add the wine, tomatoes, peas, pepper and salt, stir, cover and cook on high for 15-minutes. Release the pressure naturally for 15-minutes. Divide among serving plates. Serve warm!

Nutritional Information per serving:
Calories: 212 Fat: 46g Fiber: 1g Carbs: 13g Protein: 34g

178. Stuffed Squid
Cooking Time: 20 minutes4
Servings:
Ingredients:

- 14-ounces dashi stock
- 4 squid, tentacles separated and chopped
- 1 cup cauliflower rice, cooked
- 2 tablespoons sake
- 1 tablespoon mirin
- 1 teaspoon Truvia
- 4 tablespoons soy sauce

Directions:
In a bowl, mix cauliflower rice, tentacles, stuff the squid with mix. Place the stuffed squid into your instant pot, add the soy sauce, Truvia, mirin, sake, stir and cover. Cook on high for 15-minutes. Release pressure fast, divide squid on plates. Serve warm!

Nutritional Information per serving:
Calories: 223   Fat: 27g   Fiber: 1g   Carbs: 9g   Protein: 29g

179. Seafood Masala
Cooking Time: 15 minutes
Servings: 4
Ingredients:

- 1 ½ tablespoons red chili powder
- 17-ounces squid
- ¼ teaspoon mustard seeds
- 1 small ginger pieces, grated
- 3 tablespoons olive oil
- 4 garlic cloves, minced
- 5 small coconut pieces, shredded
- ¼ teaspoon turmeric
- 2 cups water
- Salt and black pepper to taste

Directions:
In your instant pot, mix the chili powder, squid, turmeric, water, salt, pepper and cook on high for 15-minutes. In your food processor, mix ginger with garlic, ginger, coconut, cumin and pulse. Heat up a pan with the oil over medium-high heat. Add the mustard seeds, and toast them for 2-minutes and remove from heat. Release the pressure on instant pot naturally for 10-minutes. Transfer the squid and its liquid to the pan with mustard seeds. Add the coconut paste as well. Cook for a few minutes, divide among serving plates. Serve warm!

Nutritional Information per serving:
Calories: 216   Fat: 26g   Fiber: 1g   Carbs: 5g   Protein: 23g

180. Mediterranean Octopus Dish
Cook Time: 15 minutes   **Servings: 5**
Ingredients:

- 2 rosemary sprigs
- 2 teaspoons oregano, dried
- 1 octopus, prepared
- 4 thyme sprigs
- 1 small yellow onion, chopped
- 3 tablespoons olive oil

- 1 teaspoon black peppercorns

For the Marinade:
- 4 cloves garlic, minced
- 2 thyme sprigs
- 1 sprig of rosemary

- Juice from ½ a lemon

- Juice from ½ a lemon
- Pinch of sea salt and black pepper

Directions:

In your instant pot, mix the octopus with 2 rosemary sprigs, 4 thyme sprigs, juice from ½ a lemon, peppercorns, oregano, onion, olive oil, pinch of salt. Stir, cover and cook on low for 10-minutes. Release the pressure naturally for 10-minutes. Transfer the octopus to a cutting board, cool down and chop, then put in a bowl. Mix the octopus pieces with juice from ½ lemon, ¼ cup oil, 1 rosemary sprig, 2 thyme sprigs, salt and pepper, set aside for 1 hour. Place the marinated pieces on a preheated grill over medium-high heat, cook for 3-minutes on each side. Serve with the marinade drizzled on top. Serve warm or cold!

Nutritional Information per serving:

Calories: 206 Fat: 24g Fiber: 1g Carbs: 11g Protein: 28g

181. Portuguese Seafood Stew

Cook Time: 15 minutes

Servings: 4

Ingredients:

- 1 big octopus, prepared
- 1 cup red wine
- 1 cup white wine
- ½ cup olive oil
- 2 garlic cloves, minced
- 1 yellow onion, finely chopped
- 4 potatoes, peeled, cut into quarters
- 1 tablespoon tomato paste

- ½ bunch parsley, chopped
- 1 tablespoon paprika
- 2 teaspoons pepper sauce
- 1 teaspoon hot sauce
- 2 tablespoons olive oil
- ½ cup sunflower oil
- Sea salt and black pepper to taste

Directions:

In a bowl, mix the red and white wine with water, sunflower oil, pepper sauce, tomato paste, hot sauce, paprika, parsley, salt and pepper, stir. Add the octopus, toss and coat, keep in the fridge for a day. Add the olive oil to your instant pot, and heat it using the sautė mode. Add the potatoes and onions, stir and cook for 3-minutes. Add the octopus and its marinade to instant pot, stir and cook on high for 8-minutes. Release pressure using quick-release. Divide among serving bowls. Serve hot!

Nutritional Information per serving:

Calories: 267 Fat: 30g Fiber: 3g Carbs: 16g Protein: 22g

182. Instant Pot Gumbo

Cook Time: 25 minutes
Servings: 10

Ingredients:

- 1 cup green bell pepper, chopped
- 1 cup yellow onion, chopped

- ¾ cup coconut oil
- 1 and ¼ cup almond flour

- 3 bay leaves
- 2 tablespoons peanut oil
- A pinch of cayenne pepper
- 24 shrimps, peeled and deveined
- 24 crawfish tails
- 24 oysters
- 2 cups chicken stock
- 1 teaspoon thyme, dried
- 1 lb. sausage, chopped
- 1 teaspoon celery seeds
- ½ teaspoon onion powder
- ½ teaspoon garlic powder
- 6 plum tomatoes, chopped
- ½ cup celery, chopped
- ½ lb. of crabmeat
- Sea salt and black pepper to taste

Directions:
In a pan heat the coconut oil over medium-high heat, add flour, stir very well, cook for 4-minutes and take off heat. Set your instant pot to the sauté mode, add the peanut oil and heat it. Add onion, peppers, celery, and garlic, stir and sauté for 10-minutes. Add stock, sausage, tomatoes, cayenne, onion powder, garlic powder, bay leaves, thyme, celery seeds, paprika, stir and cook for 3-minutes. Add the flour mix, crawfish, crabmeat, salt, pepper, shrimp, oysters, stir, cover and cook on high for 15-minutes. Release pressure naturally for 10-minutes. Divide among serving bowls. Serve warm!

Nutritional Information per serving:
Calories: 253 Fat: 24g Fiber: 2g Carbs: 16g Protein: 31g

183. *Easy to Prepare Octopus*
Cook Time: 35 minutes
Servings: 6
Ingredients:
- 2 lbs. octopus, head discarded, tentacles separated
- 2 lbs. sweet potatoes
- 1 bay leaf
- 2 tablespoons olive oil
- 5 tablespoons vinegar
- 2 tablespoons parsley, chopped
- 3 garlic cloves, minced
- ½ teaspoon of peppercorns
- Sea salt and black pepper to taste

Directions:
Add some water to your instant pot, add the sweet potatoes, cover and cook them on high for 15-minutes. Release the pressure naturally for 10-minutes. Transfer the sweet potatoes to a bowl, cool down and peel and chop them. Clean your instant pot, add some more water, octopus, bay leaf, 1 garlic clove, peppercorns, salt, cover and cook on high for 20-minutes. Release the pressure again naturally for 10-minutes. Drain the octopus, chop and add this to the bowl of potatoes. In a different bowl, mix the rest of the garlic with vinegar, oil, pepper, salt, and whisk well. Add this to your salad, sprinkle parsley, toss to coat. Divide among serving bowls. Serve warm.

Nutritional Information per serving:
Calories: 247 Fat: 36g Fiber: 2g Carbs: 14g Protein: 32g

184. Shrimp Risotto
Cook Time: 20 minutes
Servings: 4
Ingredients:

- 1 lb. shrimp, peeled and deveined
- 2 tablespoons white wine
- ¾ cup parmesan, grated
- ½ cup parsley, chopped
- 2 garlic cloves, minced
- 3 cups chicken stock
- 1 yellow onion, chopped
- 1 cup cauliflower rice, cooked
- 4 tablespoons butter
- Sea salt and black pepper to taste

Directions:
Set your instant pot on the sauté mode, add half of the butter, and heat it up. Add the garlic, onion, and cook and stir for 4-minutes. Add the cooked cauliflower rice, stir and cook for 1-minute more. Add 2 cups of stock, wine a pinch of salt and pepper. Set on high for 10-minutes cook time. Release the pressure naturally for 10-minutes. Add the shrimp, the remaining stock, and switch the pot to Simmer mode. Cook everything for 5-minutes, add cheese, the rest of the butter, parsley and stir. Divide among serving plates. Serve warm!

Nutritional Information per serving:
Calories: 292   Fat: 29g   Fiber: 1g   Carbs: 12g   Protein: 37g

---

185. Flounder & Shrimp
Cook Time: 5 minutes
Servings: 4
Ingredients:

- 1/2 lb. shrimp, peeled and deveined and cooked
- 2 lbs. flounder
- 4 lemon wedges
- 2 tablespoons butter
- ½ cup water
- Sea salt and black pepper to taste

Directions:
Put the water in your instant pot and place the steamer basket inside. Add the fish into the basket, season with a dash of salt and black pepper. Cover and cook on high for 10-minutes. Release the pressure using the quick-release. Divide the fish among serving plates, and leave to cool down. Clean your instant pot, add butter and set it on the sauté mode. Add the shrimp, salt and black pepper, stir and cook for a few seconds. Divide onto serving plates next to fish. Drizzle with butter all over, and serve with lemon wedges. Serve room temperature!

Nutritional Information per serving:
Calories: 282   Fat: 16g   Fiber: 1g   Carbs: 1.4g   Protein: 34g

186. Italian Shrimp Scampi

Cook Time: 5 minutes   **Servings: 4**

Ingredients:

- 1 lb. shrimp, peeled, deveined, and cooked
- 1 garlic clove, minced
- 10-ounces canned tomatoes, chopped
- 1 tablespoon parsley, chopped
- 1/3 cup water
- 1 cup parmesan, grated
- 1/3 cup tomato paste
- ¼ teaspoon oregano, dried
- 2 tablespoons olive oil
- Zucchini pasta for serving

Directions:

Set your instant pot to the sauté mode, add the oil and heat it up. Add the garlic and cook it for 2-minutes. Add the tomato paste, water, tomatoes, shrimp, oregano, parsley, stir cover and cook on high for 3 minutes. Release the pressure using the quick-release. Divide among serving plates on top of a bed of zucchini pasta. Garnish the tops with parmesan. Serve warm!

Nutritional Information per serving:

Calories: 272   Fat: 12g   Fiber: 2g   Carbs: 1.7g   Protein: 36g

187. Spicy Shrimp

Cook Time: 10 minutes   **Servings: 4**

Ingredients:

- 18-ounces shrimp, peeled and deveined
- 2 green chilies, halved lengthwise
- 2 onions, chopped
- 1 small ginger piece, grated
- Cauliflower rice already cooked for serving
- 1 teaspoon turmeric
- ½ tablespoon mustard seeds
- 3-ounces mustard oil
- Dash of sea salt

Directions:

Place the mustard seeds in a bowl, add water, leave aside for 10-minutes. Drain them and blend in your blender. In another bowl, mix shrimp, mustard oil, turmeric, mustard paste, onions, salt, chilies, and ginger, stir. Transfer this to your instant pot, cover and cook on low for 10-minutes. Release the pressure using quick-release. Divide among serving plates. Serve warm with rice!

Nutritional Information per serving:

Calories: 264   Fat: 14g   Fiber: 3g   Carbs: 1.7g   Protein: 35g

188. Special Shrimp Dish

Cook Time: 4 minutes   **Servings: 4**

Ingredients:

- 1 lb. shrimp, peeled and deveined
- 1 cup chicken stock
- 2 tablespoons soy sauce
- 1 teaspoon Truvia
- ¾ cup unsweetened pineapple juice
- ½ lb. pea pods

- 3 tablespoons vinegar

Directions:

In your instant pot combine, shrimp, pea pods, stock, vinegar, soy sauce, Truvia, pineapple juice, and stir well. Cover the pot and cook on high for 4-minutes. Release the pressure using quick-release. Divide among serving bowls. Serve warm!

Nutritional Information per serving:

Calories: 252   Fat: 15g   Fiber: 1g   Carbs: 1.6g   Protein: 23g

---

189. Creole Shrimp

Cook Time: 25 minutes   **Servings: 4**

Ingredients:

- 1 cup shrimp, cooked, peeled and deveined
- 2 teaspoons vinegar
- 1 cup tomato juice
- 1 yellow onion, chopped
- 2 tablespoons olive oil
- 1 cup celery, chopped
- ½ teaspoon Truvia
- 1 teaspoon chili powder
- 1 cup of cauliflower rice, cooked
- Dash of sea salt

Directions:

Set your instant pot to the sauté mode, add the oil and heat it up. Add the onion, celery, stir and sauté them for 2-minutes. Add the salt, vinegar, chili powder, rice, Truvia, shrimp, stir and cook on high for 3-minutes. Release the pressure using quick-release. Divide among serving plates. Serving warm!

Nutritional Information per serving:

Calories: 258   Fat: 17g   Fiber: 2g   Carbs: 1.8g   Protein: 37g

---

190. Shrimp Stew

Cook Time: 15 minutes   **Servings: 3**

Ingredients:

- 2 lbs. shrimp, peeled and deveined
- 1 lb. tomatoes, peeled, chopped
- 4 tablespoons olive oil
- A dash of sea salt
- 4 sweet potatoes, peeled, cubed
- 4 yellow onions, chopped
- 1 teaspoon coriander, dried
- 1 tablespoon watercress, chopped
- Juice from 1 lemon
- 1 teaspoon curry powder

Directions:

Put some water into your instant pot, place the steamer basket inside, add the sweet potatoes, cover and cook on high for 10-minutes. Release the pressure using quick-release. Transfer sweet potatoes to a bowl to cool down. Clean pot, add oil and set on the sauté mode. Add the onion, stir and cook for 4-minutes. Add the coriander, curry powder, and sea salt, cook for an additional 5-minutes. Add shrimp, lemon juice, sweet potatoes, tomatoes, stir. Set to high and cook for 3-minutes. Release pressure once again using quick-release. Divide among serving bowls. Serve hot!

Nutritional Information per serving:

Calories: 247   Fat: 4g   Fiber: 1g   Carbs: 1.2g   Protein: 32g

Chapter 8. Soup Instant Pot Recipes

191. *Turkey & Carrot Soup*
Cook Time: 15 minutes   **Servings: 3**
Ingredients:

- 5-ounces of turkey breast, chopped into pieces
- 2 carrots, sliced
- 3 cups chicken broth
- 2 tablespoons cilantro, chopped
- Sea salt and white pepper to taste

Directions:
Add all the ingredients into your instant pot and secure the lid. Press the Manual mode and set for a cook time of 35-minutes. Release the pressure naturally for 15-minutes. Divide among serving bowls. Serve hot!

Nutritional Information per serving:
Calories: 116   Fat: 22.5g   Carbs: 9g   Protein: 15g

192. *Fish Soup*
Cook Time: 45 minutes   **Servings: 4**
Ingredients:

- 6-ounces of mackerel fillets
- 4 cups fish stock
- 1 teaspoon rosemary, fresh, chopped
- ½ lb. tomatoes, peeled, diced
- ¼ cup sweet corn
- ½ cup wheat groats, soaked
- ½ cup kidney beans, soaked
- 2 tablespoons olive oil
- Sea salt and pepper to taste

Directions:
Grease the stainless-steel insert for your instant pot with olive oil. Press the sauté mode and add the tomatoes. Cook for 4-minutes, stir occasionally. Add the rosemary, fish stock, corn, wheat groats, beans, a pinch of salt. Close the lid and set the steam release handle. Press Manual and set for a cook time of 30-minutes. To release pressure, use the quick-release. Open the lid and add the mackerel fillets. Close lid again and press the Fish button, and cook for 10-minutes.

Nutritional Information per serving:
Calories: 464   Fat: 21g   Carbs: 3.9g   Protein: 29g

193. Turkey & Black Bean Soup

Cook Time: 55 minutes   **Servings: 4**

Ingredients:

- 6-ounces turkey, chopped
- 1 cup black beans, dried
- 1 onion, chopped
- 1 garlic clove, minced
- 3 cups water
- 1 carrot, chopped
- ½ tablespoon olive oil
- Sea salt and black pepper to taste

Directions:

Set your instant pot to the sauté mode, and add the oil and heat. Add the onions, and carrots for 5-minutes. Add the garlic and cook for one minute more. Stir in the remaining ingredients, except the salt and pepper. Close the lid, select Manual, setting and cook on high for 45-minutes. Allow the pressure to release naturally for 10-minutes. Season with salt and pepper. Divide into serving bowls. Serve hot!

Nutritional Information per serving:

Calories: 90   Fat: 8g   Carbs: 1.3g   Protein: 10g

194. Chicken & Spinach Soup

Cook Time: 5 minutes   **Servings: 6**

Ingredients:

- 1 lb. chicken, cut into chunks
- 4 scallions, chopped
- ½ onion, chopped
- 1 bulb fennel, chopped
- 2 cups chicken broth
- 1 cup spinach
- 3 garlic cloves, minced
- Sea salt and black pepper

Directions:

Place all the ingredients into your instant pot. Select Soup, and cook for 30-minutes. Allow pressure to release naturally for 10-minutes. Divide into serving bowls. Serve warm!

Nutritional Information per serving:

Calories: 181   Fat: 23g   Carbs: 6g   Protein: 25g

195. Chicken Soup with Noodles

Cook Time: 40 minutes   **Servings: 4**

Ingredients:

- 1 lb. chicken meat, cut in pieces
- 4 cups chicken broth
- ½ cup soup noodles
- Parsley for garnish
- Sea salt and black pepper to taste
- 1 cup of baby spinach, chopped
- 1 large carrot, peeled, sliced

Directions:

Sprinkle the chicken bites with salt, and place them into the instant pot. Pour the chicken broth, over the chicken, carrot, spinach, and close the lid. Set the steam release handle. Press Soup and cook for 20-minutes. Press the Cancel and release the pressure naturally for 10-minutes. Add the soup noodles and cook for 5 more minutes on the Soup setting.

Release the pressure again naturally for 10-minutes. Divide into serving bowls. Add black pepper and parsley for garnish. Serve hot!

Nutritional Information per serving:

Calories: 285   Fat: 31g   Carbs: 7g   Protein: 38g

196. *Creamy Sausage & Kale Soup*

Cook Time: 25 minutes   ***Servings: 6***

Ingredients:

- 1 lb. Italian sausage, sliced
- 3 potatoes, cubed
- 1 onion, chopped
- 1 cup heavy cream
- 2 cups kale, chopped

- ¼ cup water
- 4 garlic cloves, minced
- 1 ½ cups chicken broth
- 4 bacon slices, chopped
- 1 tablespoon olive oil

Directions:

Set your instant pot to the sauté mode, add the oil and heat it. Add the bacon and cook until crispy. Transfer to a plate. Add the onions to your instant pot and cook for 3-minutes. Add the garlic and cook for 1 more minute. Add the sausage and cook for 3 more minutes. Stir in potatoes, water and kale. Close the lid and select the Manual setting and cook for 3-minutes on high pressure. Release the pressure naturally for 10-minutes. Stir in the heavy cream, and season with salt and pepper. Divide into serving bowls. Serve warm!

Nutritional Information per serving:

Calories: 500   Fat: 35g   Carbs: 3.5g   Protein: 28g

197. *Pork Soup*

Cook Time: 55 minutes   ***Servings: 4***

Ingredients:

- 4 pork chops with bones
- 2 tablespoons soy sauce
- 1 tablespoon cayenne pepper
- 1 teaspoon chili and garlic powder
- 2 tablespoons olive oil

- 2 celery stalks, diced
- 2 onions, diced
- 2 bay leaves
- 3 medium carrots, sliced

Directions:

Set your instant pot to the sauté mode, add the oil and heat it. Add the onions, cook for 3-minutes. Add the carrots, celery, chili pepper, and cook for another 8-minutes and give it a good stir. Press the Keep Warm/Cancel button then add the pork chops, garlic powder, bay leaves, and soy sauce. Pour in the broth, and seal the lid. Set to Manual mode for 35-minutes. Release the pressure using the quick-release. Divide among serving bowls. Serve warm!

Nutritional Information per serving:

Calories: 259   Fat: 52g   Carbs: 2.9g   Protein: 47g

198. Chicken Soup with Eggs
Cook Time: 35 minutes
Servings: 6
Ingredients:

- 1 lb. chicken breast, boneless, skinless, chopped
- 2 carrots, peeled and sliced
- 2 onions, chopped
- 4 cups water
- 2 tablespoons almond flour
- 3 tablespoons olive oil
- 3 egg yolks
- 2 teaspoons cayenne pepper
- 3 small potatoes, peeled, chopped

Directions:

Set your instant pot to the sauté mode, add the oil and heat it. Add the onions, and cook them for 2-minutes. Add the remaining ingredients and seal the lid. Press the Soup button and release the pressure naturally.

Nutritional Information per serving:

Calories: 340   Fat: 15g   Carbs: 2.3g   Protein: 26g

Chapter 9. Marinades & Sauces

199. Garlic with Lemon Marinade
Cook Time: 2 minutes   **Servings: 1**
Ingredients:

- 3 tablespoons of olive oil
- 2 tablespoons of lemon juice
- 1 tablespoon lemon zest
- 1 teaspoon garlic, crushed
- Salt and pepper to taste

Directions:
Set your instant pot to sautė mode, add the oil and heat it. Add the rest of the ingredients and cook for 2-minutes, stir to combine. Allow to cool. Keep refrigerated until ready to use marinade.

Nutritional Information per serving:
Calories: 112   Fat: 21.0g   Carbs: 1.4g   Protein: 3.3g

200. Bourbon Marinade
Cook Time: 2 minutes   **Servings: 1**
Ingredients:

- 1 teaspoon cayenne pepper
- 1 tablespoon sugar or 1 teaspoon Truvia
- 2 tablespoons of bourbon
- 2 tablespoons soy sauce

Directions:
Set instant pot to sautė mode, add in all ingredients and cook for 2-minutes, stirring often. Allow to cool and store in fridge until ready to use marinade.

Nutritional Information per serving:
Calories: 132   Fat: 21.6g   Carbs: 12g   Protein: 4.1g

201. Asian-Inspired Marinade
Cook Time: 2 minutes   **Servings: 1**
Ingredients:

- 2 tablespoons soy sauce
- 2 tablespoons rice wine vinegar
- 2 tablespoons sesame oil
- 2 teaspoons ginger, fresh, grated

Directions:
Set your instant pot to sautė mode, add oil, and heat it. Add remaining ingredients and cook for 2-minutes, stir to combine. Allow to cool and keep in the fridge until ready to use.

Nutritional Information per serving:
Calories: 121   Fat: 11.2g   Carbs: 1.6g   Protein: 3.3g

202. Spicy Orange Marinade
Cook Time: 2 minutes   **Servings: 1**
Ingredients:

- 3 tablespoons olive oil
- 1 teaspoon red pepper flakes
- 1 tablespoon cilantro, fresh, chopped
- 1 tablespoon orange marmalade
- 2 tablespoons orange juice

Directions:

Set your instant pot to sauté mode, add the oil and heat it. Add the remaining ingredients and cook for 2-minutes, stirring often. Allow to cool. Store in fridge until ready to use.

Nutritional Information per serving:

Calories: 123   Fat: 7.5g   Carbs: 1.5g   Protein: 4.2g

203. Olive & Lemon Moroccan Sauce

Cook Time: 5 minutes   **Servings: 1 ½ cups**

Ingredients:

- 1 tablespoon butter
- Salt and pepper to taste
- 1 tablespoon parsley, fresh, chopped
- The juice of 1 lemon
- 1 bay leaf
- 1 stick of cinnamon
- 1 teaspoon coriander, ground
- 1 teaspoon cumin, ground
- 1 cup vegetable soup
- ½ cup green olives, chopped
- 4 garlic cloves, crushed

Directions:

Set your instant pot to the sauté mode, add the garlic cloves and olives into pot, and cook for 1-minute. Add to pot the soup, along with sliced lemon. Also add cinnamon stick, cumin, coriander and bay leaf, stir. Cook for an additional 4-minutes. Remove the bay leaf and cinnamon stick. Stir in the lemon juice and parsley. Add salt and pepper to taste along with butter, and stir. Serve warm.

Nutritional Information per serving:

Calories: 109   Fat: 11.4g   Carbs: 1.6g   Protein: 4.1g

204. Spicy Peanut Sauce

Cook Time: 5 minutes   **Servings: 1 ½ cups sauce**

Ingredients:

- 1 cup coconut milk
- ½ cup tamari or soy sauce
- 2 tablespoons brown rice vinegar
- ¼ cup smooth peanut butter
- ¼ cup of water
- 1 tablespoon ginger, fresh, grated
- 1 tablespoon cornstarch
- 2 tablespoons spicy chili sauce

Directions:

Combine all the ingredients and blend in a food processor. Pour the mixture into your instant pot, that you have set to sauté mode. Cook the mix for 5-minutes, stirring often.

Nutritional Information per serving:

Calories: 115   Fat: 8.2g   Carbs: 1.1g   Protein: 3.3g

205. Spicy Orange Sauce

Cook Time: 4 minutes

Servings: 1 ½ cups sauce

Ingredients:

- Half a cup orange juice
- 2 teaspoons toasted sesame oil
- ¼ cup lemon juice
- ½ cup tamari sauce
- 1/3 cup brown rice vinegar
- ½ cup brown sugar
- 4 garlic cloves, crushed
- A pinch of red pepper flakes

Directions:

In a small bowl mix all the ingredients, except the cornstarch and water. Add the cornstarch and water into another bowl. Add the sauce into your instant pot with the dish you are cooking. Set your instant pot on sauté mode, and cook for 4-minutes. Add the cornstarch mix into pot to thicken sauce.

Nutritional Information per serving:

Calories: 114 Fat: 11.3g Carbs: 1.2g Protein: 3.3g

206. Classic Stir-Fry Sauce

Cook Time: 5 minutes

Servings: 1 ½ cups sauce

Ingredients:

- ¼ cup cold water
- 1 tablespoon cornstarch
- A pinch of red pepper flakes
- 1 tablespoon ginger, ground
- 1 tablespoon garlic, crushed
- 1 tablespoon agave nectar
- 1 tablespoon toasted sesame oil
- 3 tablespoons brown rice vinegar
- ½ cup vegetable soup
- ½ cup tamari or soy sauce

Directions:

Mix all the ingredients in a bowl, except for water and cornstarch. In a separate bowl mix the cornstarch and water. Set your instant pot to the sauté mode, add in the sauce mixture, and cook for 5-minutes, stirring often. Add some of the cornstarch mixture to thicken the sauce. Serve warm.

Nutritional Information per serving:

Calories: 106 Fat: 11.5g Carbs: 4g Protein: 4.2g

207. Sorghum Steak Wet Rub

Cook Time: 3 minutes

Servings: 10 cups of wet rub

Ingredients:

- Hot sauce to taste
- Salt and pepper to taste
- 2 ¼ cups balsamic vinegar
- 2 ¼ cups Dijon mustard
- 3 1/3 cups of Worcestershire sauce
- 4 and a half cups tomato sauce
- 6 cups boiling water
- 6 cups raisins
- 3 cups orange juice
- 1 cup sorghum

Directions:

Place the raisins in a bowl of water and allow them to sit for 5-minutes to allow them to plump up. Add the remaining ingredients to food processor and puree until smooth. Set your instant pot to sauté mode, add the puree mixture to instant pot, and cook for 3 minutes. Season to taste with salt, pepper and hot sauce, add in the drained raisins to sauce, stir well. Allow sauce to cool then use the rub on your meat as required.

Nutritional Information per serving:
Calories: 113   Fat: 21.2g   Carbs: 4g   Protein: 4.1g

208. *Orange & Nutmeg Poultry Rub*

Cook Time: 4 minutes   ***Servings: 1 cup of rub***
Ingredients:

- ¼ teaspoon cloves
- ¼ teaspoon nutmeg
- 1 tablespoon black pepper
- 2 tablespoons orange zest
- 2 tablespoons brown sugar
- 2 tablespoons ginger, ground
- 1 cup water

Directions:
Set your instant pot to the sauté mode, add all the rub ingredients to pot, and cook for 4-minutes, stirring often. Allow rub to cool, then store in fridge until ready to use.

Nutritional Information per serving:
Calories: 114   Fat: 6.2g   Carbs: 1.2g   Protein: 3.1g

209. *Creole Rub*

Cook Time: 3 minutes   ***Servings: 1 cup rub***
Ingredients:

- ¼ cup Cajun seasoning
- 1 tablespoon hot pepper sauce
- 1 ½ tablespoons garlic, crushed
- ½ cup onion, minced
- ½ cup Creole mustard
- ½ cup water

Directions:
Set your instant pot to sauté mode, add all the ingredients into pot, and cook for 3-minutes, stir often. Allow mix to cool before applying it to meat as required.

Nutritional Information per serving:
Calories: 102   Fat: 8.2g   Carbs: 1.3g   Protein: 4.2g

210. *Ketchup with Cola Marinade*

Cook Time: 2 minutes   ***Servings: 1 ½ cups marinade***
Ingredients:

- 1 garlic clove, crushed
- 1 teaspoon paprika
- 2 teaspoons yellow mustard, dry
- 2 tablespoons olive oil
- 3 tablespoons apple cider vinegar
- 3 tablespoons brown sugar
- 1 cup tomato ketchup
- 1 cup cola

Directions:

Set your instant pot to the sauté mode, add the oil and heat it. Add the rest of the ingredients, and cook for 2-minutes, stirring often. Allow marinade to cool then keep in the fridge until ready to use.

Nutritional Information per serving:
Calories: 103   Fat: 31.6g   Carbs: 1.7g   Protein: 4.1g

---

211. *Spicy Beer Wings Marinade*
Cook Time: 3 minutes   ***Servings: 1 cup of marinade***
Ingredients:

- Half a cup of beer
- 1 tablespoon of olive oil
- 2 whole jalapenos
- 7 garlic cloves, crushed
- 2 whole habaneros
- ½ a teaspoon of paprika
- 1 teaspoon garlic powder
- 2 teaspoons salt

Directions:
Add all the ingredients into food processor, and blend until finely chopped. Set your instant pot to sauté mode, add the mixture into pot, and cook for 3-minutes, while stirring to combine. Allow the mixture to cool. Put mixture in container and place in fridge to chill for a few hours. Remove from fridge add to a plastic lock bag along with chicken wings. Lock the bag and shake it to make sure the wings are coated with marinade sauce. Place the bag in the fridge overnight, shake every couple of hours. Remove your wings from the fridge about 10-minutes before you want to cook them.

Nutritional Information per serving:
Calories: 111   Fat: 31.6g   Carbs: 15g   Protein: 4.2g

---

212. *Coffee Steak Marinade*
Cook Time: 5 minutes   ***Servings: 1 ½ cups marinade***
Ingredients:

- A teaspoon of salt
- A teaspoon of black pepper
- A teaspoon of red pepper flakes
- 2 fresh rosemary sprigs
- 3 garlic cloves, chopped
- 4 tablespoons maple syrup
- 1 cup of black coffee, cooled

Directions:
Set your instant pot to the sauté mode, add all the ingredients and cook for 5-minutes, stir often. Allow marinade to cool, place in a container and refrigerate for 2-hours. Marinate steak in mixture for 2 hours in the fridge. After 1 hour turn the steak over during the marinating process. Once steak is fully marinated cook it to taste and serve hot.

Nutritional Information per serving:
Calories: 110   Fat: 21.7g   Carbs: 10g   Protein: 3.3g

213. Blue Cheese Sauce

Cook Time: 5 minutes   **Servings:** 1 cup sauce

Ingredients:
- 1 cup of blue cheese
- 1 cup of double cream

Directions:
Set your instant pot to the sauté mode, add the ingredients and cook for 5-minutes, stirring often. Serve warm. This sauce is great with beef, pork or chicken dishes.

Nutritional Information per serving:
Calories: 108 Fat: 21.3g Carbs: 2.1g Protein: 5.3g

214. Classic Pepper Sauce

Cook Time: 15 minutes
Servings: 2 cups of sauce
Ingredients:
- 2 cups evaporated milk
- 2 tablespoons Worcestershire sauce
- 2 teaspoons black ground pepper
- 2 teaspoons green peppercorns
- 1 tablespoon olive oil

Directions:
Set your instant pot to the sauté mode, and oil and heat it. Add your choice of meat and cook for 5-minutes browning all sides. Remove the meat and set aside. Add sauce ingredients into pot and blend them with the meat juices in pot. Cook for an additional 5-minutes, stirring often. Add the meat back into the pan and continue to sauté for another 5-minutes. Serve hot.

Nutritional Information per serving:
Calories: 117 Fat: 11.5g Carbs: 1.6g Protein: 4.2g

215. Chili Sauce with Tomato

Cook Time: 7 minutes   **Servings:** 2 cups sauce

Ingredients:
- ½ cup water
- Pinch salt and pepper
- 2 tablespoons tomato puree
- 1 cup sugar
- 6 red birds eye chilies, thinly sliced
- 4 red chilies, thinly sliced
- 2 capsicums, peeled and deseeded
- 2 onions, roughly chopped
- 6 large tomatoes, ripe
- 1 tablespoon olive oil

Directions:
Peel all the tomatoes and remove stalks, and slice into quarters. Set your instant pot to the sauté mode, add oil and heat it. Add onions and cook for 2-minutes. Add tomatoes, chili seeds, capsicum and chilies, cook for 5-minutes stirring often. Use a stick blender to make the sauce runny, and stir in the sugar, stir. This sauce works great with red meat dishes.

Nutritional Information per serving:
Calories: 116 Fat: 21.3g Carbs: 1.6g Protein: 4.1g

216. Classic Cream & Garlic Sauce
Cook Time: 5 minutes   **Servings: 1 ½ cups sauce**
Ingredients:

- 1 tablespoon corn flour
- ¾ cup of cream
- 1 beef stock cube
- 1 cup water

- 1 tablespoon garlic steak seasoning
- 1 tablespoon of garlic powder
- 4 garlic cloves, crushed
- 1 tablespoon olive oil

Directions:
Set your instant pot to the sauté mode, add oil and heat it. Peel and crush up garlic cloves and add to instant pot, cook for 2-minutes. Add water, and crumble in the stock cube. Add seasoning and garlic powder into pot and stir. Pour in the cream and stir again, cook for an additional 3-minutes. Add in corn flour and stir, this will thicken sauce. This sauce goes great with steak or surf and turf. Serve hot.

Nutritional Information per serving:
Calories: 114   Fat: 11.4g   Carbs: 1.8g   Protein: 3.3g

217. Marinara Sauce
Cook Time: 15 minutes
Servings: 1 cup sauce
Ingredients:

- ¼ cup oregano, fresh, chopped
- Salt and pepper to taste
- 3 tablespoons of olive oil
- 1 head of roasted garlic

- ½ cup red wine
- 2 (28-ounce) cans of plum tomatoes
- 1 red onion, large, finely chopped

Directions:
Set your instant pot to the sauté setting, add oil and heat it. Add the red onions, and cook for 2-minutes. Add garlic into pot and cook for an additional 3-minutes. Add the wine to pot and mix well. Add half of the oregano, salt and pepper, stir. Add the tomatoes and rest of ingredients into pot. Set the pot to Manual setting on high with a cook time of 10-minutes. When the cook time is competed, release the pressure naturally for 10-minutes. Allow the sauce to cool for 30-minutes. Add sauce to blender and blend until smooth. Leave in fridge overnight. Serve with pasta.

Nutritional Information per serving:
Calories: 219   Fat: 11.6g   Carbs: 2.1g   Protein: 4.2g

218. Brown Sauce
Cook Time: 5 minutes
Servings: 1 ½ cups sauce
Ingredients:

- ½ cup red wine
- 2 tablespoons butter

- 2 tablespoons almond flour
- 1 cup beef stock

- Salt and black pepper to taste
- ½ teaspoon parsley, dried

Directions:

After you have browned your meat in instant pot, remove it from pot. Set pot on sauté mode, and add the butter and heat it. Add flour and whisk sauce in pot. Add wine and seasonings and whisk. When sauce thickens, pour it over your meat and serve hot.

Nutritional Information per serving:

Calories: 218   Fat: 11.2g   Carbs: 1.2g   Protein: 3.3g

---

219. *Veloute Sauce*

Cook Time: 10 minutes   **Servings: 1 cup sauce**

Ingredients:

- 1 cup shallots, chopped finely
- ½ cup white mushrooms, diced
- ½ cup white wine
- Salt and black pepper to taste
- 1 cup of chicken stock
- 2 tablespoons butter
- 1 tablespoon almond flou

Directions:

Set your instant pot to the sauté mode, add the butter and heat it. Add flour and stir. Add the shallots and cook for 2-minutes. Add the mushrooms and cook for an additional 3-minutes, stir. Add the stock, white wine, seasonings, stir and cook for another 5-minutes, stirring often. Serve sauce hot, pour over protein dishes or even just vegetables.

Nutritional Information per serving:

Calories: 218   Fat: 11.5g   Carbs: 1.9g   Protein: 4.6g

---

220. *Tuscan Style Meat Sauce*

Cook Time: 28 minutes   **Servings: 2 cups sauce**

Ingredients:

- 1 lb. tomatoes, peeled, and chopped
- 1 tablespoon tomato paste
- ½ cup red wine vinegar
- 4-ounces pork, ground
- 4-ounces beef, ground
- 1 large stalk of celery, minced
- 1 carrot, large, minced
- 1 onion, minced
- 2 tablespoons extra-virgin olive oil
- Salt and pepper to taste

Directions:

Set your instant pot to the sauté mode, add the oil and heat it. Add the pork and beef, and cook for 5-minutes, stirring and browning on all sides. Remove meat from pan and set aside. Add onions, carrots, celery to pot and cook for 3-minutes. Add the wine, tomatoes, seasoning, stir to combine. Add the meat back into pot. Close the lid to pot and set on Manual, on low with a cook time of 20-minutes. When the cook time is completed, release the pressure naturally for 10-minutes. Serve hot over pasta.

Nutritional Information per serving:

Calories: 262   Fat: 12.8g   Carbs: 2.6g   Protein: 25.3g

221. Indonesian Soy Sauce

Cook Time: 15 minutes
Ingredients:

Servings: 1 cup sauce

- 2/3 cup soy sauce
- 8 bay leaves

- 2/3 cup brown sugar
- 1 cup water

Directions:
Set your instant pot to the sauté mode, and add the ingredients into it, and stir. Blend well to combine, and cook for 5-minutes. Set the pot to Manual setting on low, for a cook time of 10-minutes. When the cook time is completed, release the pressure naturally for 10-minutes. Serve sauce hot or cold.

Nutritional Information per serving:
Calories: 131   Fat: 1.1g   Carbs: 1.1g   Protein: 3.2g

222. Sweet Coney Island Sauce

Cook Time: 30 minutes
Ingredients:

Servings: 1 cup sauce

- ¼ cup ketchup
- ¼ teaspoon hot pepper sauce
- ¼ teaspoon celery seed
- 1 teaspoon Worcestershire sauce
- 1 tablespoon water

- 2 tablespoons white sugar or 1 tablespoon Truvia
- 2 tablespoons cider vinegar
- 2 tablespoons prepared mustard
- 1 lb. ground beef
- 2 tablespoons olive oil

Directions:
Set your instant pot to sauté mode, add oil and heat it. Add the ground beef, brown on all sides, stir and cook for 10-minutes. Add in the rest of the ingredients and stir. Close lid and set to Manual setting on low for 20-minute cook time. When the cook time is completed, release the pressure naturally for 10-minutes. Serve warm over pasta.

Nutritional Information per serving:
Calories: 223   Fat: 11.7g   Carbs: 2.4g   Protein: 23.9g

223. Wine Sauce

Cook Time: 15 minutes
Ingredients:

Servings: 1 ½ cup sauce

- 1 cup plain bread crumbs
- 2 tablespoons red wine vinegar
- 1 cup beef stock
- 3 tablespoons parsley, dried

- 2 cloves garlic, minced
- 2 shallots, minced
- 2 yellow onions, minced
- ¼ cup white wine

Directions:
Set to sauté mode, add all the ingredients into pot and stir, cook for 5-minutes. Set to Manual on low for a cook time of 10-minutes. When the cook time is completed, release the pressure naturally for 10-minutes. Serve this wine sauce over boneless pork butt roast.

Nutritional Information per serving:
Calories: 172 Fat: 12.8g Carbs: 2.6g Protein: 4.3g

---

224. Mustard Cream Sauce
Cook Time: 5 minutes   **Servings: 1 cup sauce**

Ingredients:
- 2 tablespoons heavy cream
- 2 tablespoons coarse-grain mustard
- 1 cup chicken stock

Directions:
Set your instant pot to the sauté mode, add the ingredients for sauce and cook for 5-minutes, stirring often. Serve this sauce over cooked steaks. Serve hot.

Nutritional Information per serving:
Calories: 182 Fat: 11.7g Carbs: 2.2g Protein: 4.1g

---

225. Green Pea Sauce
Cook Time: 5 minutes   **Servings: 1 ½ cups sauce**

Ingredients:
- ½ cup canned evaporated milk
- 1 tablespoon olive oil
- 1 medium onion, finely diced
- 2/3 cup frozen peas
- 1 cup vegetable broth
- Salt and pepper to taste

Directions:
Set your instant pot to the sauté mode, add the oil and heat it. Add the onion and cook for 2-minutes, stir. Add the garlic, and stir. Add the peas into pot and stir to thaw. Add the evaporated milk, and vegetable stock. Close the lid to pot and set pot to Manual on low with a cook time of 3-minutes. When the cook time is complete, release the pressure using quick-release. Add salt and pepper to taste and stir. Serve warm over honey-glazed ham.

Nutritional Information per serving:
Calories: 153 Fat: 9.6g Carbs: 2.1g Protein: 4.2g

---

226. Mexican Mole Sauce
Cook Time: 10 minutes   **Servings: 1 cup sauce**

Ingredients:
- 1 (4-ounce) can diced green chile peppers
- 1 (10.75-ounce) can condensed tomato soup
- 1/8 teaspoon of garlic, minced
- 1 teaspoon cilantro, dried
- 1 teaspoon cumin, ground
- 1 tablespoon unsweetened cocoa powder
- ¼ cup onion, finely chopped
- 2 tablespoons olive oil

Directions:
Set your instant pot to the sauté mode, add the oil and heat it. Add the onion, and cook for 2-minutes, stir. Mix in cumin, cilantro, garlic, and cocoa powder. Stir in the tomato soup

and green peppers. Close lid and set to Manual on low with a cook time of 8-minutes. When the cook time is completed, release the pressure using quick-release. Transfer to gravy boat and serve warm over red meat dishes.

Nutritional Information per serving:
Calories: 186 Fat: 11.3g Carbs: 2.0g Protein: 4.2g

---

227. Thai-Style Peanut Sauce with Honey

Cook Time: 4 minutes   **Servings: 1 cup sauce**

Ingredients:

- 1 tablespoon ginger, fresh, minced
- 1 teaspoon red pepper flakes, crushed
- 2 teaspoons garlic cloves, minced
- 2 tablespoons sesame oil
- 2 tablespoons extra-virgin olive oil
- 2 tablespoons rice vinegar
- 3 tablespoons soy sauce
- 1 tablespoon crunchy peanut butter
- ¼ cup smooth peanut butter
- ½ cup honey

Directions:
Set your instant pot to the sauté mode, add olive and sesame oil, heat them. Add honey, peanut butter, rice vinegar, soy sauce, ginger, red pepper flakes, stir and cook for 4-minutes. Serve warm over favorite Thai dish.

Nutritional Information per serving:
Calories: 163   Fat: 21.6g Carbs: 2.4g Protein: 6.2g

---

228. Ginger-Tamarind Sauce

Cook Time: 20 minutes   **Servings: 3 cups sauce**

Ingredients:

- ½ teaspoon red pepper, ground
- 2 tablespoons coriander powder
- 1 tablespoon tamarind paste
- 2 cups water
- 2 tablespoons ginger, chopped, fresh
- 1 cup onion, chopped
- 1 teaspoon mustard seed
- 1 tablespoon olive oil
- ½ teaspoon chile powder

Directions:
Set your instant pot to sauté mode, add the oil and heat it. Add in the mustard seeds, and cook for 2-minutes. Add in the onion, and ginger, stir and cook for an additional 3-minutes. Stir in the tamarind paste, water and season with chile powder, red pepper, coriander and salt. Close the lid to pot and set to Manual on low for a cook time of 15-minutes. When the cook time is completed, release the pressure naturally for 15-minutes. Stir in ½ pound of fish of choice such as cod fillets, cubed into 1-inch pieces, and set on sauté until the fish is cooked through, stir often. Serve warm.

Nutritional Information per serving:
Calories: 189 Fat: 21.2g Carbs: 2.1g Protein: 3.2g

229. Enchilada Sauce

Cook Time: 13 minutes

Ingredients:

- Garlic powder to taste
- ¼ cup tomato sauce
- 2 cups water

Servings: 2 cups sauce

- ¼ cup chili powder
- 2 tablespoons almond flour
- 2 tablespoons olive oil

Directions:

Set your instant pot to the sauté mode, add the oil and heat it. Stir in the flour and cook for 1-minute. Add in the chili powder and cook for another minute. Add in the water, tomato sauce, seasonings and whisk to remove lumps. Cover with lid and set pot to Manual setting on low with a cook time of 11-minutes. When the cook time is completed, release the pressure naturally for 10-minutes. Serve warm over enchilada dish.

Nutritional Information per serving:

Calories: 173   Fat: 21.2g   Carbs: 2.1g   Protein: 4.4g

---

230. Creamy White Wine Sauce

Cook Time: 5 minutes

Ingredients:

- 1 teaspoon parsley, dried
- 1 teaspoon salt
- 2 tablespoons almond flour

Servings: 1 cup sauce

- ¾ cup white wine
- 1 cup heavy whipping cream

Directions:

Set your instant pot to the sauté mode, add the sauce ingredients and stir to combine. Cook the sauce for 5-minutes stirring often, bring to a boil. Serve warm over favorite chicken dish.

Nutritional Information per serving:

Calories: 166   Fat: 21.2g   Carbs: 2.4g   Protein: 4.4g

---

231. Sweet & Sour Sauce

Cook Time: 5 minutes

Ingredients:

- 1 teaspoon cornstarch
- ¼ cup water
- 3 drops red food coloring
- 1 teaspoon garlic powder
- 4 teaspoons soy sauce
- ½ cup ketchup

Servings: 2 cups sauce

- 2 teaspoons monosodium glutamate (MSG)
- ½ cup pineapple juice
- 1 cup white sugar or 2 tablespoons Truvia
- 1 cup distilled white vinegar

Directions:

Set your instant pot to the sauté mode, add vinegar and sugar and stir to combine. Add pineapple juice, monosodium glutamate, ketchup, garlic powder, salt, soy sauce, and cook for 5-minutes and stir. Add in the food coloring and mix. In a small cup mix water and cornstarch, slowly add to mixture in pot until you get desired consistency. Serve warm with favorite pork or chicken dish.

Nutritional Information per serving:
Calories: 206 Fat: 12.6g Carbs: 2.9g Protein: 4.8g

---

232. Mustard Sauce

Cook Time: 3 minutes   **Servings: 1 cup sauce**

Ingredients:
- ¼ cup sour cream
- ¼ cup Dijon mustard
- 2 teaspoons cornstarch
- 1 cup chicken broth

Directions:
Set your instant pot to the sauté mode, add the sauce and cornstarch, whisk and cook for 1-minute. Add in mustard, and sour cream, stirring often, and cooking for an additional 2-minutes. Serve warm over favorite chicken dish.

Nutritional Information per serving:
Calories: 209 Fat: 12.5g Carbs: 2.4g Protein: 3.8g

---

233. Cranberry Sauce

Cook Time: 10 minutes   **Servings: 1 ½ cups sauce**

Ingredients:
- 1 cinnamon stick
- ½ teaspoon salt
- 1 tablespoon apple cider vinegar
- ¼ cup white sugar
- 1/3 cup seedless raspberry jam
- 2/3 cup water
- 1 cup pitted prunes, quartered
- 1 (12-ounce) package of fresh or frozen cranberries

Directions:
Set your instant pot to the sauté mode, combine prunes, water, cranberries, raspberry jam, sugar, salt, vinegar, and cinnamon stick in pot, stir occasionally for 3-minutes. Close lid and set to Manual setting on low with a cook time of 10-minutes. When the cook time is completed, release the pressure naturally for 10-minutes. Allow sauce to cool then transfer to container and place in fridge for at least 3 hours before serving. Serve warm or cold over favorite poultry dish.

Nutritional Information per serving:
Calories: 213 Fat: 12.8g Carbs: 2.8g Protein: 4.7g

---

234. Rum Sauce

Cook Time: 5 minutes   **Servings: 1 ½ cups sauce**

Ingredients:
- 3 tablespoons white or dark rum
- 1 cup milk
- ½ cup sugar or 1 tablespoon Truvia
- 1 tablespoon cornstarch
- 2 tablespoons butter

Directions:

Set your instant pot to the sauté mode, add the sugar and cornstarch and mix. Add in the butter. Pour in the milk and stir often cooking for 5-minutes. Transfer sauce into a bowl and stir in the rum. Serve warm.

Nutritional Information per serving:
Calories: 210   Fat: 12.8g   Carbs: 7g   Protein: 4.5g

Conclusion

I do hope that you have enjoyed reading my recipe book, as much as I have enjoyed writing it. I hope that my recipe collection will offer you some new and healthy options to add to your daily diet.

The best thing that I discovered while writing this book is that your meals do not have to be tasteless and boring to be healthy. Within these pages is a wide selection of recipes that are full of wonderful flavors that will have your tastebuds tingling with delight while at the same time offering you good nutritious meals.

To further reduce your sugar intake, I would suggest replacing any sugars in my recipe collection with the wonderful "Truvia" a calorie-free natural sweetener that comes from the Stevia plant, native to South America. I wish you immense success in adding new and healthier meal choices to your diet—that are not only good for you but taste amazing!

Made in the USA
San Bernardino, CA
04 March 2018